Principia Astrologia de Financial

Course 2

2017

M. G. BUCHOLTZ, B.Sc., MBA

Wood Dragon Books

Box 1216, Regina, Saskatchewan, Canada, S4P 3B4

www.wooddragonbooks.com

ISBN# 978-0-9953342-4-3

Copyright 2017 Malcolm Bucholtz, B.Sc., MBA

Printed in Canada

Contents

Figures and Tables

Acknowledgements

To the many traders and investors who at a visceral level
suspect there is more to the financial market complex than
P/E ratios and analyst recommendations. You are correct.
There is more. Your open mind tells you there is much more.
The markets are in fact rooted in astronomical and
astrological timing. This learning course will add a whole new
dimension to your market activities.

Disclaimer

All material provided herein is based on material gleaned from mathematical and astrological publications researched by the author to supplement his own trading. This publication is written with sincere intent for those who actively trade and invest in the financial markets and who are looking to incorporate astrological phenomena and esoteric math into their market activity. While the material presented herein has proven reliable to the author in his personal trading and investing activity, there is no guarantee the material herein will continue to be reliable into the future. The author and publisher assume no liability whatsoever for any investment or trading decisions made by readers of this book. The reader alone is responsible for all trading and investment outcomes and is further advised not to exceed his or her risk tolerances when trading or investing on the financial markets.

Recommended Readings

The Bull, the Bear and the Planets, M.G. Bucholtz, (iUniverse, USA, 2013)

The Lost Science, M.G. Bucholtz, (iUniverse, USA, 2013)

The Cosmic Clock, M.G. Bucholtz (Wood Dragon Books, Canada, 2016)

The Universal Clock, J. Long, (P.A.S. Publishing, USA,)

McWhirter Theory of Stock Market Forecasting, L. McWhirter, (Astro Book Company, USA, 1938)

The Universe Within, N. Turok, (House of Anansi Press, Canada, 2012)

A Theory of Continuous Planet Interaction, Tony Waterfall, *NCGR Research Journal, Volume 4, Spring 2014*, pp67-87.

Introduction

In the Introduction to Principia Astrologia, Course 1, I wrote of my two theories of what drives the financial markets.

I wrote of the Sun projecting its energy into space and that energy flux coming to manifest itself on Earth. We mortals, made up mostly of water, have an electrical system in our bodies. This variably changing solar energy flux impacting our bodily circuitry is what stimulates emotion and drives the markets.

I then shared with you my second theory that the markets are manipulated from deep within by savvy operators who make their power and influence known at key astrological events.

You have now read the material from Course 1 and started to apply it to stocks and commodities that you follow. What are your thoughts at this point on Astrology? Is it being used to manipulate the markets? Or are we frail humans impacted by cosmic energy that causes our emotions to shift from buy to sell and back again? Much to ponder, indeed.

In Course 2, I am going to gently lead you deeper into the mysteries of Astrology.

I will introduce you to Louise McWhirter. In the 1930s, Louise McWhirter identified an 18.6 year cyclical correlation between the general state of the American economy and the position of the North Node of Moon. Her methodology also extends to include an analysis of the Moon passing by key points of the 1792 natal birth horoscope of the New York Stock Exchange. As well, she identified a correlation between price movement of a stock and those times when transiting Sun, Venus, Mercury, Mars, Jupiter and Saturn made hard aspects to the natal Sun position in natal birth horoscope of a stock or commodity.

I will then introduce you to the equally mysterious Giacomo Albano and his use of classical Astrology in predicting the general tone of the markets into the future.

I will then introduce you to a third mysterious figure who in 1921 called himself Professor Watson. He crafted a white paper in which he demonstrated how to use cosine mathematics and Fourier series mathematics to arrive at a plot that illustrates price inflection points on commodities, stocks and indices. This math will challenge your mind, but in the end it will open your mind.

As always, I must caution that when applying Astrology to trading and investing, it is vital at all times to be aware of the price trend. There are many ways of observing trend. My personal experience has shown me that the chart indicators developed by J. Welles Wilder are very effective at identifying trend changes. In particular, the Directional Movement Indicator (DMI) and the Volatility Stop are two indicators that should be taken seriously. As a trader and investor, what you are looking for is a change of trend that aligns to an astrological event. When you see the trend change, you should take action. Whether that action is implementing a long position, a short position or just tightening up on a stop loss will depend on your personal appetite for risk and on your investment and trading objectives. Astrology is not about trying to blindly take action at each and every astrological event that comes along. Not all events are powerful enough to induce a change of trend. Hence, that is why I advise to be alert at each astrological event and to keep your eye open for changes in trend.

I sincerely hope after you have applied the material in this second learning Course to your trading and investing activity, you will further embrace Astrology and the mysteries and hidden patterns of the financial markets.

1. The McWhirter Method

In Course 1, I pointed out that in the 1930s there were some who briefly made their connection to Financial Astrology known by writing a book. One of these people was Louise McWhirter. Very little is known about Louise McWhirter, except that she was an Astrologer and lived in New York City somewhere in the neighborhood near Carnegie Hall. In 1937 she wrote the book *McWhirter Theory of Stock Market Forecasting*. What became of her after 1937? Did she personally know W.D. Gann? Was she consulting to the big market players of the day? Sadly, these are questions that I doubt I will ever find the answers to. In my travels to places as far away as the British Library in London, England to research Financial Astrology, not once did I come across any other books by her. Not once did I find any other book from her era that even mentioned her name. All of this I find to be deeply mysterious. It appears that she had her moment of fame with the release of her book. She then evidently quietly faded to the sidelines, most likely to quietly pursue her Astrology.

There are **three** components to the McWhirter approach.

The **first** component involves the transit of the North Node (also called North Node of Moon) around the Zodiac wheel. It takes 18.6 years for the Node to complete a full transit through all 12 signs of the Zodiac. When the Node moves through certain signs, the economic business cycle reaches a low point and when the Node is in certain other signs, the business cycle is at its strongest.

Recall from Course 1 of this series that the Earth and other planets orbit the Sun in a plane of motion called the Ecliptic Plane. The Earth is tilted slightly relative to this plane. If one extends the equator of the Earth out into space the result is a plane called the Equatorial Plane. By mathematical definition, two planes that are not parallel to one another must at two points intersect. To astrologers, the points of intersection are termed the North Node and South Node. In the McWhirter method, it is only the North Node that is used.

The **second** component of the McWhirter approach pertains to the New York Stock Exchange which was founded in May 1792. The McWhirter approach focuses on the Moon and its 29.5 day lunar cycle. There are several key features that one can note in the horoscope chart for the New York Stock Exchange. By studying the planetary positions in the Zodiac wheel at the time of a New Moon, one can identify additional key features. As the 29.5 day lunar cycle progresses, by watching for times when Moon and other planets make aspects to these key features, one can identify times when there is a strong probability of a short term trend change (inflection point) on the Dow Jones Average. The Dow Jones Average is comprised of 30 large cap stocks that trade on the New York Stock Exchange. The stocks that comprised this Average in McWhirter's day were different from the ones that today comprise the Average. But, her method, nonetheless, continues to work.

The **third** part of the McWhirter approach pertains to individual stocks and commodity futures. By studying the First Trade horoscope chart of a stock or commodity future, one can identify key planets and critical planetary aspects. By watching for times when the transiting Sun and various transiting planets make aspects to these key positions, one can identify times when there is a strong likelihood for a trend change.

The McWhirter approach has many subtleties and nuances. But, once you have become comfortable with the method, you will be in possession of a skill that very few other traders, investors and investment advisors have.

Ascendant and Mid-Heaven

In Course 1, you learned that as the Earth rotates on its axis once in every 24 hours, an observer situated on Earth will detect an apparent motion of the Zodiac.

To better define this motion, astrologers apply four cardinal points to the Zodiac, almost like the north, south, east and west points on a compass. As shown in Figure 1, these cardinal points divide the Zodiac into four quadrants. The east point is termed the Ascendant and is often abbreviated Asc. The west point is termed the Descendant and is often abbreviated Dsc. The south point is termed the Mid-Heaven (from the Latin Medium Coeli) and is often abbreviated MC. The north point is termed the Imum Coeli (Latin for bottom of the sky) and is abbreviated IC.

Two of these cardinal points, namely the Mid-Heaven and the Ascendant are important when using the McWhirter method. Another way to think of the Ascendant is that constellation which is on the easterly horizon at any given time. The Mid-Heaven is that constellation that is at its greatest declination in the south at a given time. The Earth rotates once in 24 hours, so therefore it stands to reason that the Ascendant takes 24 hours to travel once around the Zodiac wheel.

The New York Stock Exchange was founded May 17, 1792. Astrologers take the time of inception to be just before 8:00 am in the morning. As Figure 2 illustrates, at this morning hour, the Ascendant was at 14 degrees of the sign of Cancer. The Mid-Heaven was at 24 degrees of Pisces. Recall from Course 1 that geocentric astrology is the most common version used in the context of studying the financial markets. Look carefully at the descriptive data in the upper left corner of Figure 2 and you will see that this chart has been generated using the geocentric method.

The degree point 14 of Cancer figures elsewhere in American history too. Consider that George Washington was sworn in as the first US President on April 30, 1789. The location was New York City. The time was 9 am. The Moon at that time was passing 14 Cancer.

Consider also where the Sun was on July 4, 1776 when the Declaration of Independence was signed. Yes…14 of Cancer.

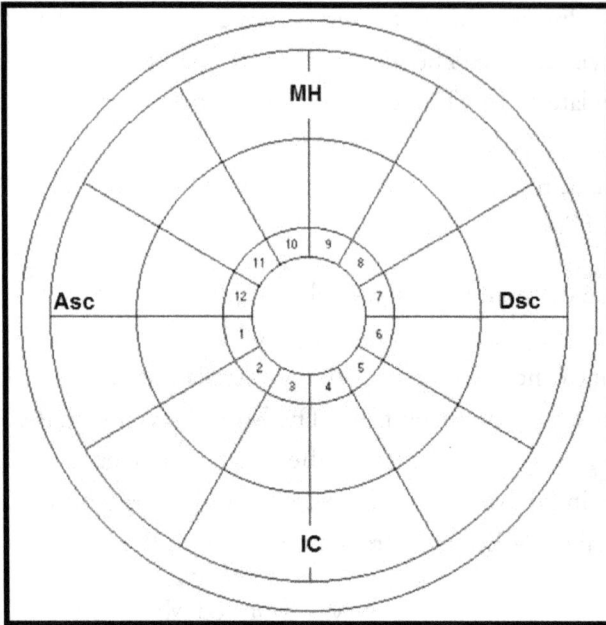

Figure 1 The Cardinal Points

Lastly, there is another peculiar account to consider involving 14 of Cancer. In the early 1500's writer Bartolome de las Casas documented the travels of Columbus on his voyage of discovery. As las Casas tells it, near mid-night on October 11, 1492 a distant flickering light was spotted. At daybreak the next day, October 12, 1492, Columbus and his party went ashore to what is today the Bahamas. And with that, the New World had been discovered. And where was the Moon late in the evening of October 11, 1492? Indeed – it was passing 14 of Cancer.

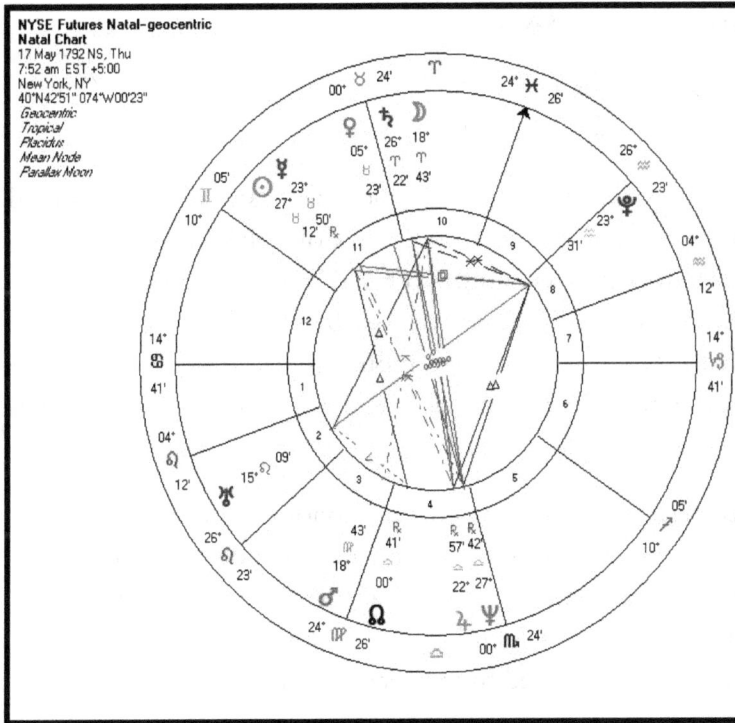

Figure 2 Birth Horoscope of the NYSE

Study Figure 2 further and you will see the Zodiac wheel is divided into twelve segments. These segments are not of equal size. In astrology software programs, there are different mathematical ways of dividing the Zodiac into its twelve segments, called Houses. If you happen to be using a software program for applying Astrology, in your program you will be presented with a drop down menu offering you the various methods for House division. The most common option for creating House division is the *Placidus* system. This system is named for 17th-century mathematician and astrologer Placidus de Titis. It is thought the Placidus system is based on 13th century Arab writings. Throughout this learning Course, I shall be using the Placidus system of House divisions, except for one component of the McWhirter method. Understanding the mathematical rigors of House divisions is not essential to your success at using Astrology to navigate the financial markets.

The 18.6 year Business Cycle

Let's start with a deeper look at the **first** component of the McWhirter method – the movement of the North Node.

McWhirter closely followed the economic forecasts of Colonel Leonard P. Ayers at the Cleveland Trust Company. Colonel Ayers was a devout student of the stock market and was revered by the American Government for his published correlations between business activity and stock market indices. One of his more famous correlations related the number of operating blast furnaces in the American steel industry to stock market tops and bottoms.

A further correlation was noted between economic activity and Astrology. Whether McWhirter was the one to identify this correlation or whether Ayers recognized it first remains unclear. Ayers, by the way, was also an avid student of Astrology. I am sure he kept that bit of information quietly concealed from his employer.

The correlation between economic activity and astrology posits that the North Node of the Moon moving through the various signs of the zodiac aligns to periods of strength and weakness in economic activity. A full journey of the North Node around the 12 signs of the Zodiac comprises one complete business cycle in the economy.

The North Node is deemed to have dampening, suppressive forces similar to that of Saturn. So, at the peak of a business cycle, these dampening forces are at a minimum and at the low point in a business cycle these dampening forces are at their strongest.

Mathematically, to an observer positioned on Earth, it appears as though the Nodes are progressing backwards in a Retrograde motion as time elapses.

In late 2016 I had an experience of my own with the 18.6 year cycle of the Node. I was fortunate enough to be able to visit Stonehenge in England. I learned that the megalithic peoples who built Stonehenge had an intimate understanding of the Moon. They were able to figure out that every 18.6 years the Moon will come back to being in alignment with the same constellation stars that it aligned to 18.6 years prior. I was awestruck when I learned this. How is it that so much knowledge came to be lost over the centuries. Why are we just now again figuring this stuff out?

Tools

As noted in Course 1, good data is the key to being able to apply Astrology to the financial markets.

To obtain a good part of this data, financial astrologers use Ephemeris Tables. For geocentric Astrology, the *New American Ephemeris for the 21st Century* is commonly used. It is available at most bookstores. For heliocentric Astrology, the *American Heliocentric Ephemeris* is a good resource. It tends to be harder to find in bookstores but on-line booksellers may have it available.

Data describing when planets are at maximum and minimum elongation, declination and at superior and inferior conjunction tends to be a bit harder to find.

Thankfully, I have discovered the US Navy (in conjunction with the UK Hydrographic Office) publishes data tables each year. You can down load the 2016 tables at the website:

http://aa.usno.navy.mil/publications/reports/ap16_for_web.pdf

The 2017 data is at the following link:

http://aa.usno.navy.mil/publications/reports/ap17_for_web.pdf

For faster data access, an excellent software program is Solar Fire Gold produced by Astrolabe (**www.alabe.com**). I also use a market platform called Market Analyst. This brilliant piece of software, (originally developed in Australia) allows the user to generate an end of day price chart and then quickly overlay various astrological aspects and occurrences onto the chart. In my not so humble opinion, all serious adherents of Financial Astrology should spend the money to acquire this software program.

Practical Exercise

Look at the data in your Ephemeris tables. Find the column containing the positional data for the Node. As you look forward in the Ephemeris from one year to the next, note which direction the Node moves. Indeed – it moves backwards (Retrograde) through the Zodiac signs.

The length of time for the Nodes to make one journey through the 12 Zodiac signs is 18.6 years. This means that every 1.55 years, the Node will enter into a different Zodiac sign.

Louise McWhirter with the help of her banking friend Colonel Ayers, was able to discern the following:

• As the Node enters Aquarius, the low point of economic activity has been reached

• As the Node leaves Aquarius and begins to transit through Capricorn and Sagittarius, the economy starts to return to normal

• As the Node passes through Scorpio and Libra, the economy is functioning above normal

• As the Node transits through Leo, the high point in economic activity has been reached

• As the Node transits through Cancer and Gemini, the economy is easing back towards normal

• As the Node enters the sign of Taurus, the economy begins to slow

- As the Node enters Aquarius, the low point of economic activity has been reached and a full 18.6 year cycle has been completed.

McWhirter further observed some secondary factors that could influence the tenor of economic activity in a **good way**, no matter which sign the Node was in at the time:

- Jupiter being 0 degrees conjunct to the Node

- Jupiter being in Gemini or Cancer

- Pluto being at a favorable aspect to the Node

McWhirter also observed some secondary factors that can influence the tenor of economic activity in a **bad way**, no matter which sign the Node was in at the time:

- Saturn being 0, 90 or 180 degrees to the Node

- Saturn in Gemini or Cancer

- Uranus in Gemini

- Uranus being 0, 90 or 180 degrees to the Node

- Pluto being at an unfavorable aspect to the Node

Practical Exercise

Look at the data in your Ephemeris. What sign is the Node in? When will the Node transition to the next Zodiac sign? Does the Node make any 0, 90 or 180 degree aspects to Saturn, Uranus, Pluto or Jupiter?

Aspects

The horoscope wheel in Figure 3 illustrates the Node in the sign of Virgo in September 2016. Node in Virgo signals that the general economy is strong. When the Node passes through Leo during part of 2017 and part of 2018, the economy according to the McWhirter method will start to ease back to more modest growth rates. In Figure 3, Node being 90 degrees to Saturn signals some pressure on the economy.

There are many ways of measuring the economy, from the Consumer Price Index to Employment Participation Rates to Housing Starts. This Saturn 90 degrees to Node aspect was in effect in September and into October, 2016. Recall what happened during the US Election campaign. Thanks to the verbiage of the campaign, voters realized the extent to which jobs were going off-shore and the extent to which job creation in America was in the low wage service sector and not the higher wage manufacturing sector. As well, statistics from the US Commerce Department show that in September 2016 overall housing starts were down sharply on a month over month basis.

A typical case of McWhirter's method in action. And by the way, when looking for these aspects, 90 degree aspects are deemed valid if the amount of separation between the two bodies is between 84 degrees and 96 degrees. Conjunction (0 degrees) and Opposition (180 degrees) are valid +/- 10 degrees. Trines (120 degrees) are deemed valid +/- 6 degrees.

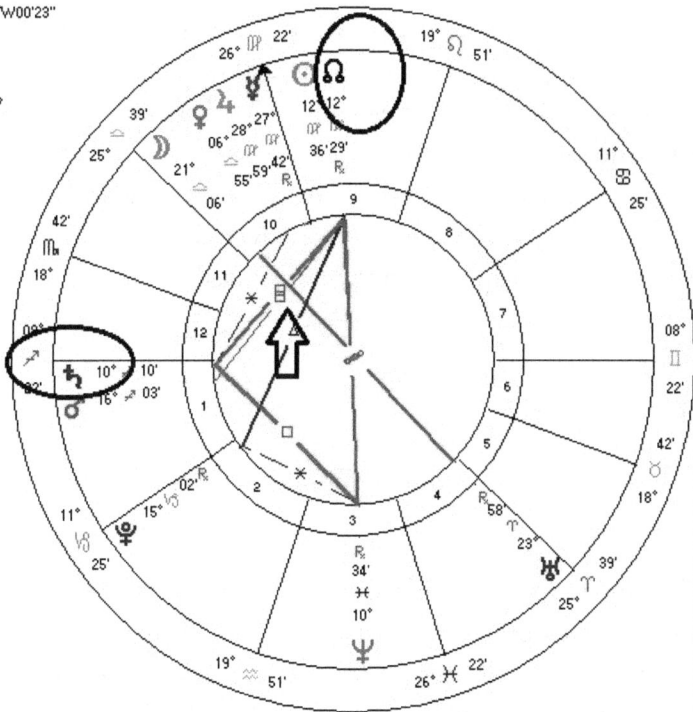

Figure 3 Node at a 90 degree aspect

When applying this part of the McWhirter method, I typically do not worry so much about the various transitory aspects between Node and other planets. I focus more on the sign the Node is in and I also focus on those times when Node transits from being in one Zodiac sign to being in another. Sometimes it helps to take a step back to better see the tenor of economic activity within an 18.6 year cycle. If I look around my community where I live, I see a major new sports stadium being built, new schools being built and a massive new highway project being completed to the tune of $1 Billion. Certainly none of these projects was being talked about when Node was leaving Aquarius several years ago.

Practical Exercise

Look at the data in your Ephemeris. What sign was the Node in as 2008 dawned? What does the McWhirter method say about Node in this sign? What did the economy do in 2008 and into 2009 as Node moved through this sign? When will the Node again start to move through Aquarius? How will you plan to safeguard yourself, your family and your investments during this transit? As an aside to this exercise, I can tell you that my wife and I are already in the planning stages for the Node coming into Aquarius in the not so distant future.

The Lunar Cycle

Let's now look at the **second** component to the McWhirter method – the lunar cycle.

Recall from your readings in Course 1, a lunar cycle is the time it takes for the Moon to completely orbit the Earth. A lunar cycle is 29.5 days as viewed from our vantage point here on Earth. To an astrologer, a lunar cycle begins at a New Moon and ends 29.5 days later at the next New Moon.

To properly work with these lunar cycles, it will help to have a software program in which you can adjust the position of the Ascendant by clicking your computer mouse. In particular, at a New Moon event each month, you will be adjusting the horoscope wheel so that Ascendant rests at 14 of Cancer. With this adjustment made, you can then proceed to analyse the horoscope.

Aspects at the New Moon

In classical astrology, each of the 12 Houses is deemed to have a planet(s) that reign powerful over that House. The expression used by astrologers is "ruler-ship". Louise McWhirter in her writings stated clearly that based on her analysis of the 1792 birth horoscope of the New York Stock Exchange, it was ruled by Mars and Neptune.

When analyzing a horoscope at a New Moon event, it is thus vital to look for 0, 90, 120 or 180 degree aspects to Mars and Neptune. It is also important to look to see where Saturn is and whether it is in any aspect to other planets. Saturn in the realm of Financial Astrology is deemed to be a heavy-weight, oppressive planet. Mars is deemed to be a fire-like, aggressive, volatile planet. Neptune is deemed to be associated with change (volatility) as is Pluto. Venus is deemed to be a positive planet as is Jupiter. Mercury can be either positive or negative and it oftentimes called the "trickster". As you have seen in your readings from Course 1, financial markets can all too often experience big volatility at Mercury Retrograde events.

One could spend the next 5 years reading books on classical Astrology and its interpretations. But, for the purposes of studying the markets with the McWhirter approach, I prefer to keep things simple.

On a horoscope, a New Moon event that is at 90 or 180 degrees to Saturn, Neptune, Uranus, Mars, Jupiter or even Venus, implies limitation, frustration, difference, accident-prone, conflict. A 0 degree aspect of New Moon to these planets will tend to herald above normal market volatility. This general tone of observation will also apply to Mars being 0, 90 or 180 degrees to Saturn, Neptune, Uranus, Jupiter and Venus. A 120 degree aspect of New Moon to these planets will be generally positive.

Practical Exercise

Using the data from an Ephemeris or from your software program, sketch or generate a horoscope wheel for August 3, 1997 using a location of New York. By clicking your mouse, adjust the position of the Ascendant so it resides at 14 of Cancer. You should have a horoscope that resembles that of the image in Figure 4.

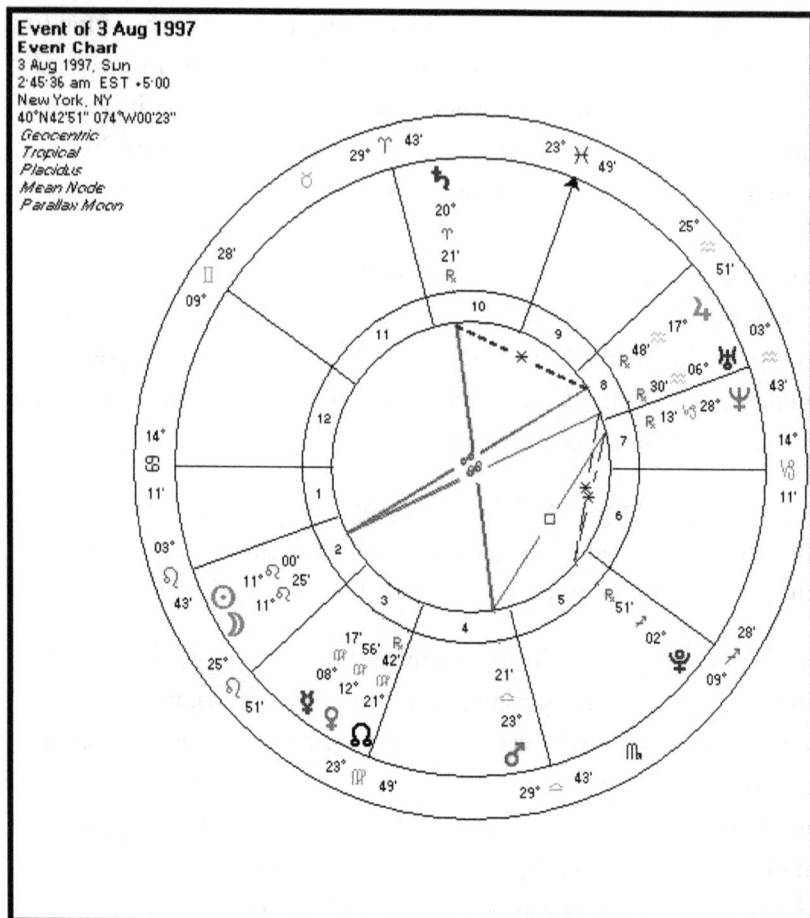

Figure 4 August 1997 New Moon

Note that the New Moon is opposite Jupiter and opposite Neptune (NYSE ruler). Note further that Mars (NYSE ruler) is opposite Saturn. Mars is also 90 degrees square to Neptune. There are no aspects to Venus or Mercury.

All in all, this horoscope appears to be charged with negative energy.

Why have I picked the date of August 3, 1997 for this analysis? Well, it turns out that the New York Exchange suffered a bout of panic at this time due to the events swirling around the Asian Currency Crisis. The price chart in Figure 5 illustrates the effect on the Dow Jones.

Had a person been using the McWhirter method on a regular basis, the negative energy apparent in the August New Moon horoscope would have hopefully convinced that person to take steps to protect his or her investment positions. Note also in Figure 5 that the Wilder Volatility Stop signalled a trend change. Note further that Mercury Retrograde followed close behind. All too often I find that a negative prospect offered up at a New Moon will also be connected to other less than positive astrological events going on as well.

The McWhirter method will never tell you how much the market will rise or fall. You have to be following the trend and you have to be alert. At this point, if you are still unsure about trend chart indicators, I encourage you to review the material from Course 1 on the Wilder Volatility Stop and the DMI.

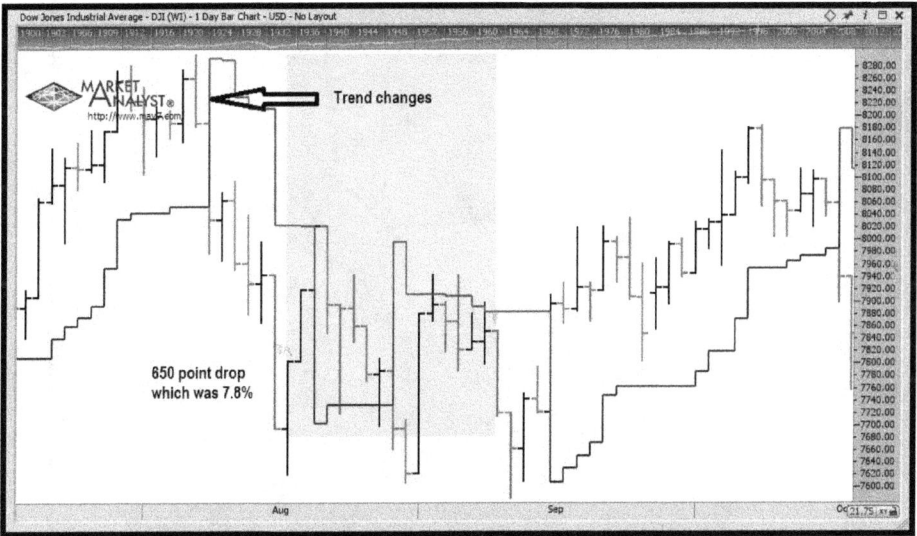

Figure 5 Asian Currency Crisis – August 1997

Practical Exercise

Using the data from an Ephemeris or from your software program, sketch or generate a horoscope wheel for October 29, 2016 using a location of New York. By clicking your mouse, adjust the position of the Ascendant so it resides at 14 of Cancer. You should have a horoscope that resembles that of the image in Figure 6.

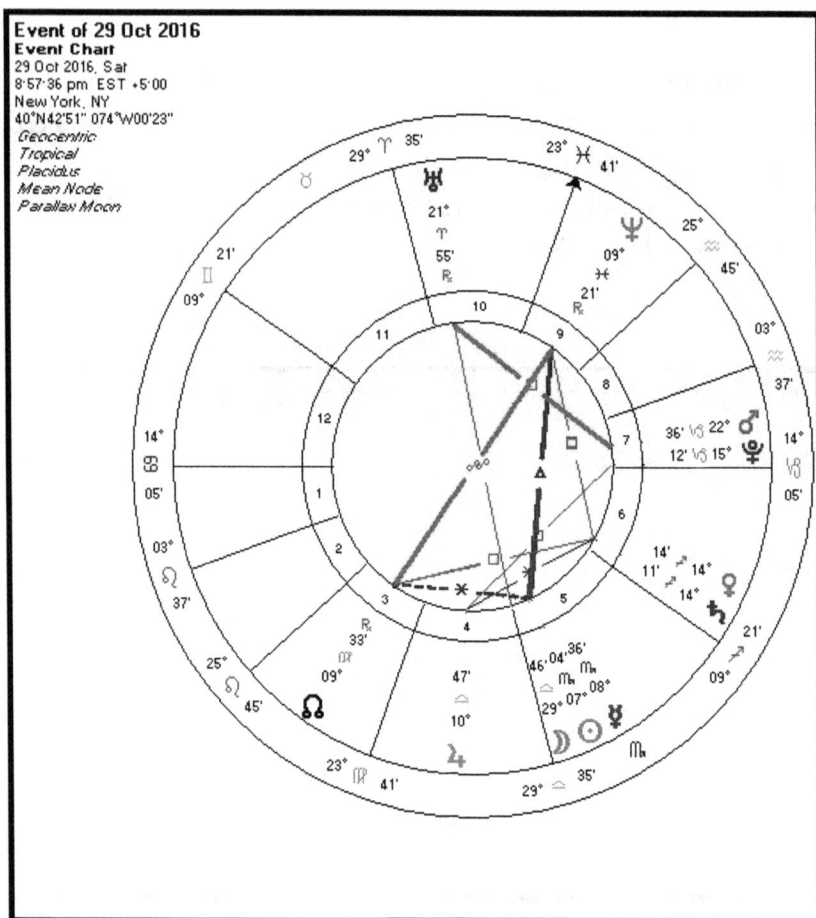

Figure 6 October 2016 New Moon

Note that Node, Neptune and Saturn/Venus together form a big right-angled triangle. In Astrology, this is called a *"T-Square"*. It generally denotes negative energy, but its effects can be softened somewhat depending on what planets it is comprised of. Note also that Node,

New Moon and Neptune (NYSE ruler) make a right-angled triangle where the New Moon is at the 90 degree apex of the triangle. This shape is called a *"Point of Thales"* and is a positive occurrence. Lastly note that Mars (NYSE ruler) is 90 degrees square to Uranus.

This chart does indicate the presence of negative energies, but the Point of Thales that involves the New Moon speaks to positive energy. Venus situated at a 0 degree aspect to heavy-weight Saturn on balance tends to soften the grumpy old Saturn as Venus is the planet of money and love.

Why have I picked this date as an example? This was the New Moon event immediately ahead of the US Presidential Election. This election had a rather unexpected outcome which initially caused the markets to decline from the New Moon date into voting day as Figure 7 shows. There was the negative energy suggested in the New Moon horoscope wheel. But, after all was said and done, the markets took on a positive tone, with the Dow Jones rising 1000 points from the Election night lows.

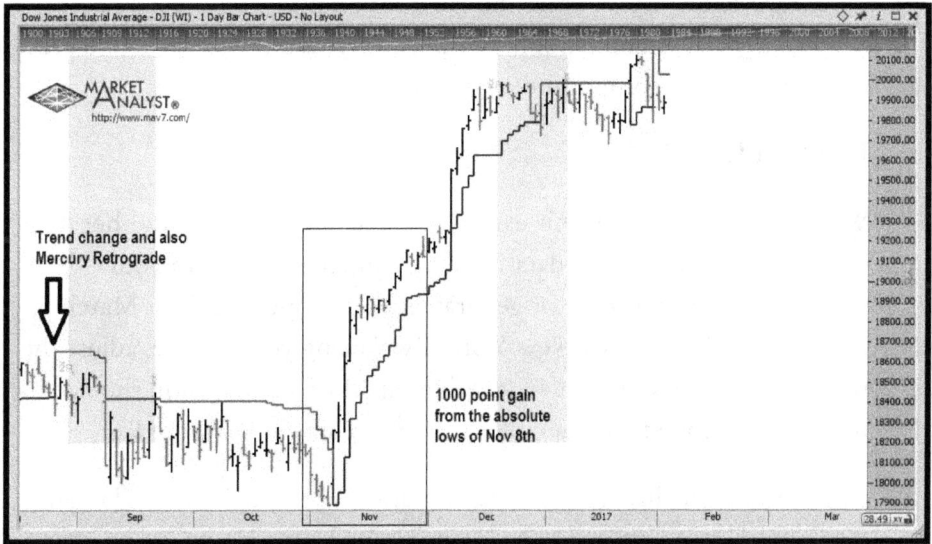

Figure 7 Dow Jones and the October 2016 New Moon

Consider now what happens if the New Moon event makes a hard aspect to that very special of locations, 14 degrees of Cancer. In January 2000 (January 14 to be exact), the Dow Jones reached a high water mark and then proceeded to record a nasty tumble.

Practical Exercise

Using the data from an Ephemeris or from your software program, sketch or generate a horoscope wheel for January 6, 2000 using a location of New York. By clicking your mouse, adjust the position of the Ascendant so it resides at 14 of Cancer. You should have a horoscope that resembles that of the image in Figure 8.

Notice that the Node has nearly finished transiting through Leo in January 2000 which was suggesting the economy had already seen its best days in the 18.6 year cycle. This in itself should have been a red flag when combined with the lofty level of the markets and the irrationally exuberant sentiment being exhibited on Wall Street.

Note further in Figure 8 that the New Moon event is in fact 180 degrees to the esteemed point 14 of Cancer. Saturn was also 90 degrees to NYSE ruler Neptune, another warning sign.

Practical Exercise

While we are looking at this early 2000 timeframe, here is another exercise to do. Using the data from an Ephemeris or from your software program, sketch or generate a horoscope wheel for March 5, 2000 using a location of New York. By clicking your mouse, adjust the position of the Ascendant so it resides at 14 of Cancer. You should have a horoscope that resembles that of the image in Figure 9.

Again, the Node has nearly finished transiting through Leo in January 2000 which was suggesting the economy had already seen its best days in the 18.6 year cycle. The recent stiff drop in the Dow Jones is telling you that trouble is brewing. But, can the markets stage a bounce-back?

Note in Figure 9 that the New Moon event is in fact a soft 60 degrees to Saturn. Aggressive Mars is softened by its 60 degree aspect to tough-guy Uranus and to money planet Venus. Jupiter is 90 degrees square Neptune. This softens Jupiter's otherwise expansive attitude, but is not a negative warning.

So, on balance, there is positive energy suggested in this horoscope. Don't forget too that Mercury is Retrograde which is highly indicative of a trend change.

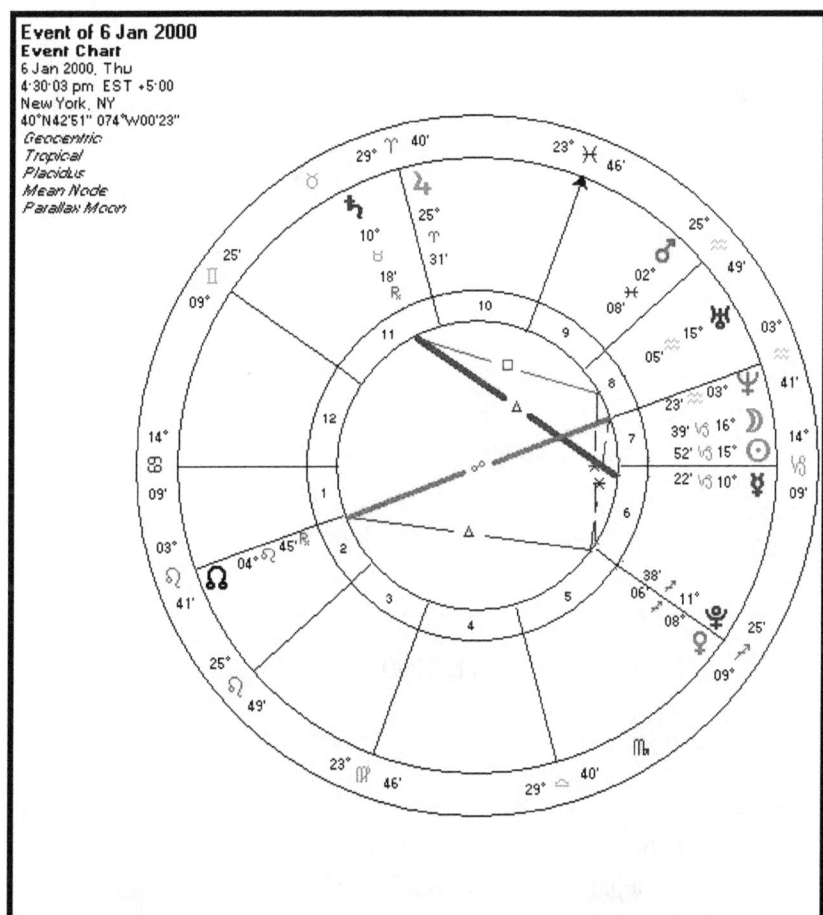

Event of 6 Jan 2000
Event Chart
6 Jan 2000, Thu
4·30·03 pm EST +5·00
New York, NY
40°N42'51" 074°W00'23"
Geocentric
Tropical
Placidus
Mean Node
Parallax Moon

Figure 8 January 2000 New Moon

33

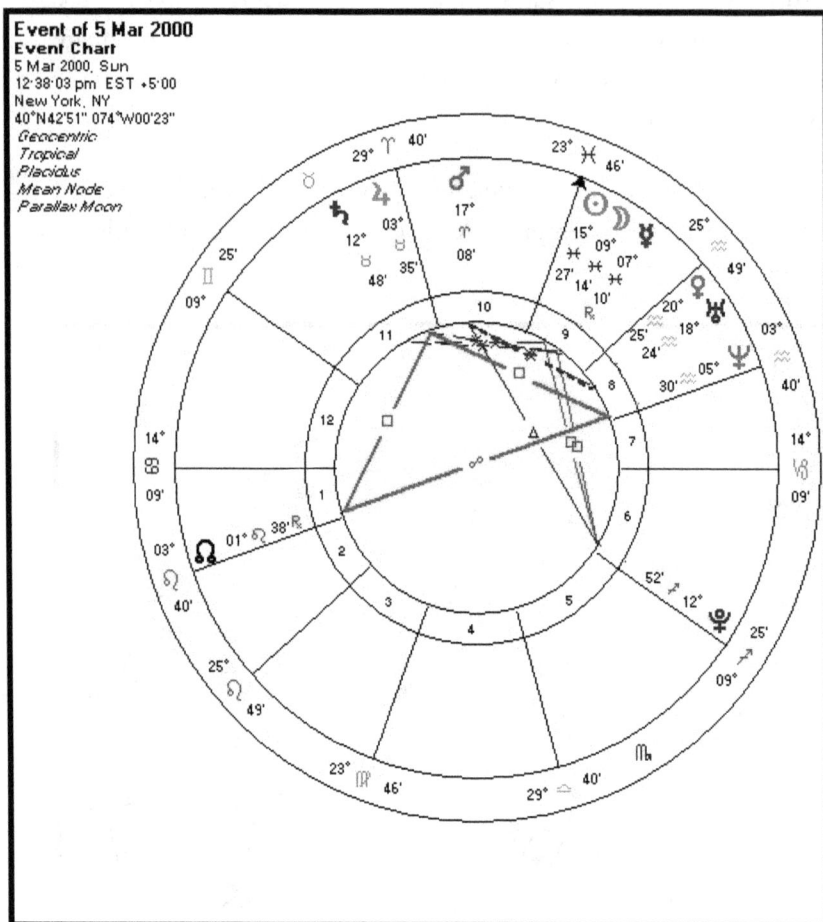

Figure 9 March 2000 New Moon

Take a look at the price chart of the Dow Jones shown in Figure 10. You can see that the January New Moon gave negative warnings and the trend did turn negative. The March New Moon gave positive energy and when combined with a Mercury Retrograde event, the result was a recovery in the market.

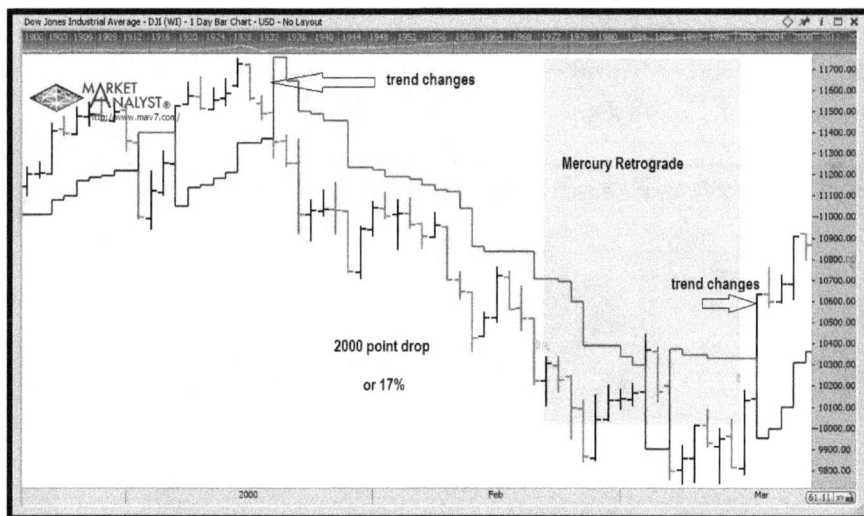

Figure 10 Dow Jones in Early 2000

Critical Points in the Lunar Cycle

Louise McWhirter took things a bit further when she demonstrated that the transiting Moon passing by certain key points in the Zodiac wheel aligned to short term inflection points on the New York Stock Exchange. The points that she focused on were the natal Ascendant point of 14 Cancer, the natal Mid-Heaven point of 24 Pisces, ruling planet Mars and ruling planet Neptune. Any time you see the word '*natal*' associated with Astrology, immediately start looking at the First Trade horoscope wheel. In this case, the natal Ascendant and Mid-Heaven are from the May 1792 NYSE horoscope.

The best way to illustrate these lunar transits is to study some examples.

To determine the dates when the transiting Moon passes these critical points, you can use your Ephemeris tables or you can generate a horoscope wheel in your software program.

The Dow Jones price chart in Figure 11 is from mid-2016 onwards and has been overlaid with those times when Moon transited past the vaunted point of 14 Cancer (NYSE natal Ascendant).

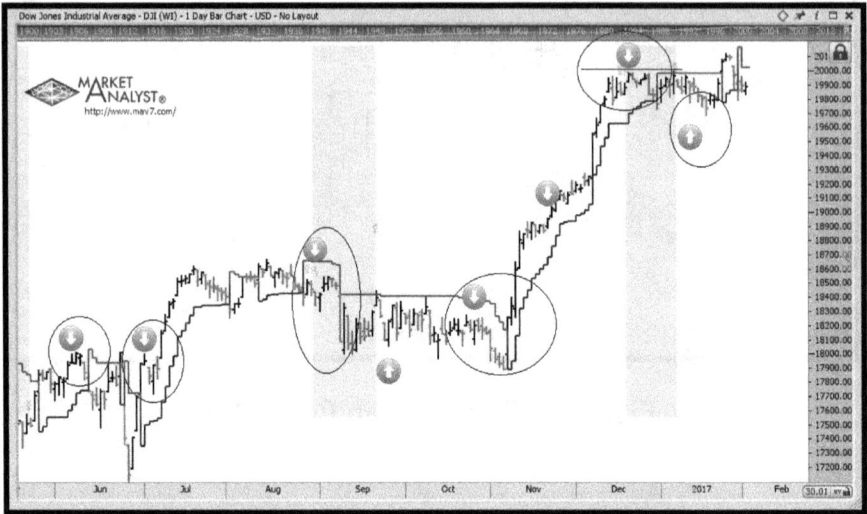

Figure 11 Dow Jones and Moon / Asc Transits

In June 2016, the Moon/natal Ascendant transit preceded a slight drop in the Dow. In July, this transit came just as the Wilder Volatility Stop was flashing a short term trend change to positive. In very late August, this transit again marked a brief tumble in the Dow as did the transit in late October. The December event capped what had been a powerful post-election rally. The January event came a few days ahead of a brief dip in the Dow.

I continue to be amazed at how Moon passing the natal Ascendant point of 14 Cancer each month all too often aligns to short term trend swings. It is almost like someone behind the curtain is manipulating the market. Or are they?

The Dow Jones price chart in Figure 12 is from mid-2016 onwards and has been overlaid with those times when Moon transited past the NYSE natal Mid-Heaven point of 24 Pisces.

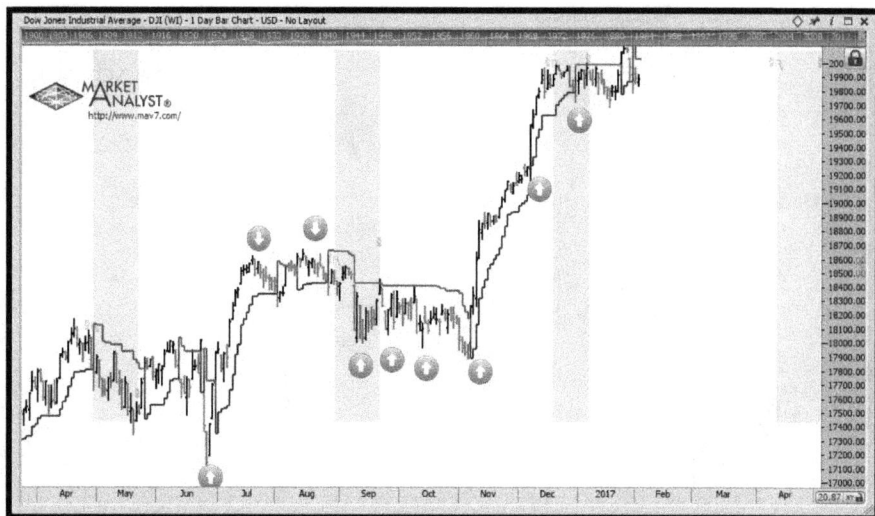

Figure 12 Dow Jones and Moon / Mid-Heaven Transits

In June 2016 the Mid-Heaven transit came as the market was probing a bottom and setting up for a re-bound. The re-bound in July ran out of steam at a Mid-Heaven transit. From September through November, the Moon passing the natal Mid-Heaven point of 24 Pisces aligned to several swing low points, including the nasty sell-off once the markets realized who the new President of the USA was going to be. In December, the 24 Pisces transit aligned to a serious burst higher in an already up-trending market.

The Dow Jones price chart in Figure 13 is from mid-2016 onwards and has been overlaid with those times when Moon transited past the planet Mars, which is one of the rulers of the New York Stock Exchange.

Again, the correlation to swing points leaves one scrambling for an explanation. Is this the cosmos at work or is there something deeper and darker going on?

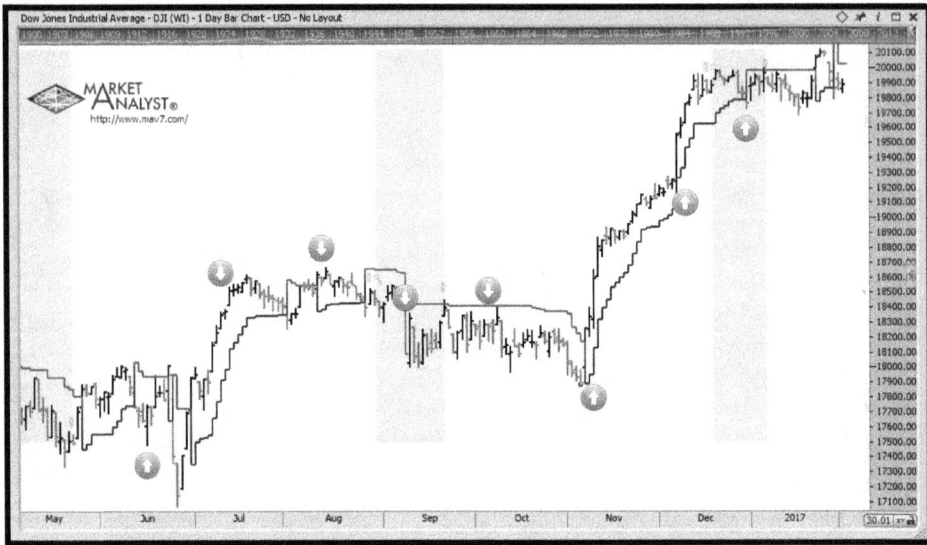

Figure 13 Dow Jones and Moon / Mars Transits

Practical Exercise

Using your Ephemeris tables, determine the dates when Moon transits the points 14 Cancer, 24 Pisces and also when Moon transits Mars and Neptune every month for, say…, the last 4 months. Next, generate some short term charts of the Dow Jones and study these transits in more detail. See how you could have taken advantage of such transits using a 30 minute or an hourly chart. Now, determine these transit dates for the next 3 months. As they occur, practice *on paper* taking advantage of them by executing hypothetical short term trades on Dow Jones futures or e-mini futures.

Let's now look at the **third** component of the McWhirter method, namely using planetary transits to gain more insight into individual stocks and commodities.

Louise McWhirter based this part of her work on the date that a stock or a commodity future contract first started trading on a recognized exchange.

If you visit my website at www.investingsuccess.ca, you will find a link to tables that give you the first trade dates of North American stocks. It has taken me quite a while to determine the dates when the various commodity futures contracts started trading and I will list these dates in this section of the Course.

What I have determined over the past several years of applying McWhirter's work is that simple is best. I look for those times when the following events happen:

- Sun makes 0, 90, 120, 180 degree aspects to natal Sun

- Mars makes 0, 90, 120, 180 degree aspects to natal Sun

- Mars makes 0, 90, 120, 180 degree aspects to natal Mars

- Mars makes 0, 90, 120, 180 degree aspects to natal Jupiter

- Transiting Saturn makes 0 and 90 degree aspects to natal Sun

- Transiting Jupiter makes 0 and 90 degree aspects to natal Sun

These events are not necessarily frequent. Earth takes 365 days to orbit the Sun. Therefore, from our vantage point here on Earth we will see Sun making a 0, 90, 120 and 180 degree aspect to a stock's natal Sun only six times a year.

Mars takes 687 days to orbit the Sun. From our vantage point here on Earth we will see Mars make various aspects to a stock's natal Sun, natal Mars and natal Jupiter only a handful of times each year.

Saturn takes 29.42 years to orbit the Sun and Jupiter takes 11.85 years. From our vantage point here on Earth, Saturn and Jupiter will make aspects to the natal Sun very infrequently. But, when these aspects do occur, they can be powerful events.

Does the McWhirter technique works for all stocks? The answer is a definite no. In order for astrology to be applied to an individual stock, that stock must be seen to be trading decent volumes every day. Stocks that have days where trading volume is low or negligible are not suitable candidates for the McWhirter method because not enough people and therefore not enough emotional energy are impacting price movement. This then rules out many of the micro-cap stocks that trade on the OTC market in the USA or on the TSX Venture Exchange in Canada. This also rules out stocks having low trading volumes because large blocks of stock are owned by passive investors who choose not to trade.

The First Trade Horoscope

As noted earlier, I would be using Placidus House divisions except for one part of the McWhirter method. McWhirter decided to create her First Trade horoscopes in a very different way. I have read her material many times over and cannot figure out why she opted for this unusual setup. She arranges the horoscope wheel so that Sun appears on the cusp of the First House. Furthermore, she arranges the horoscope so that all the Houses in the wheel are an equal 30 degrees. The location for the horoscope is the city where the stock exchange or commodity exchange is located. The time of the horoscope is the time the exchange starts trading each day (for stocks, I use 9:30 am for the NYSE and TSX, for commodities I assume 9:00-9:30 am). She then looks for patterns that may exist within the chart such as T-Squares, Trines, Kites and so on. She then pays strict attention to those times when various planets transit past natal Sun, natal Mars, natal Venus and the corner points of any patterns evident in the horoscope.

Let's look at a few examples of some stocks using McWhirter's method.

Let's start with a look at a mineral exploration company that has been trying to advance a world-class Copper mining project in Alaska. The name of the company is Northern Dynasty Mining and it first started trading in Canada on the Toronto Stock Exchange on October 30, 2007.

Figure 14 illustrates the First Trade horoscope.

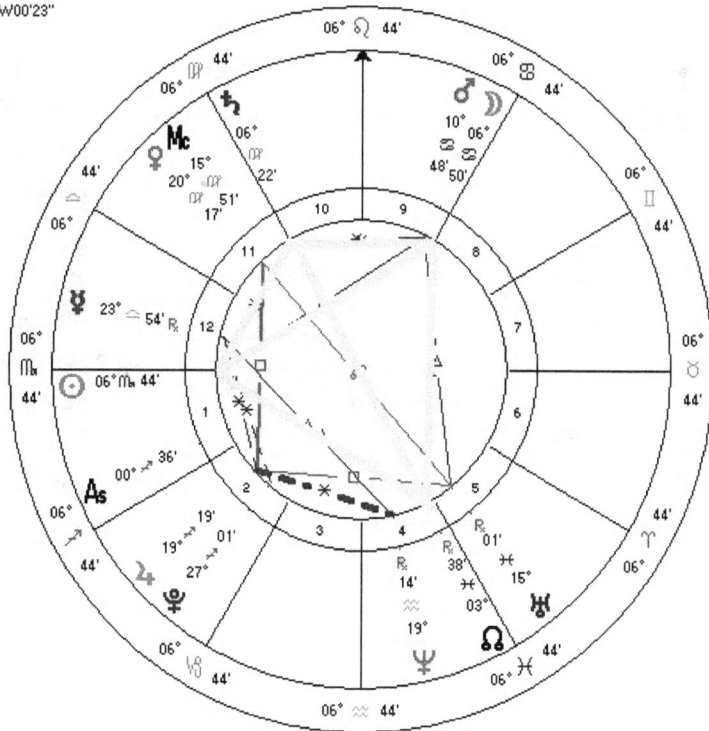

Figure 14 – Northern Dynasty Mining (TSX:NDM) First Trade Horoscope

This horoscope has been set up with Sun on the cusp of the first House, just as Louise McWhirter advises in her writings. The one thing that stands out is the peculiar shape that is drawn by connecting Sun-Saturn-Moon(Mars) – Node. This is what astrologers call a "Kite" formation. Kites are generally regarded as very positive. The take-away from this First Trade horoscope is that Northern Dynasty is a company that will survive the rigors of advancing its mining project. In fact, this is exactly what has happened. Through challenges from the Environmental Protection Agency and the Army Corps of Engineers, the company has survived. Many other companies facing similar hurdles would have failed long ago.

As an aside, in early 2008 I was in New York at a small investment event where the focus was on Canadian junior mining stocks. That is where I met the venerable financial astrologer Henry Weingarten. I had not yet discovered Financial Astrology at that point in my life, but I do recall Mr. Weingarten talking about the importance of picking the correct date to commence your stock starting to trade on an Exchange. I also recall him briefly citing Northern Dynasty as an example. Now, seeing this Kite formation in the NDM First Trade horoscope, I know exactly what he was talking about. For those that do not know of Mr. Weingarten, after 2008 he ran afoul of the Securities Exchange Commission (SEC). After a legal battle, he ended up paying a fine and the SEC found no fault with him. Truly a bizarre situation. What was really going on was that Mr. Weingarten was openly talking about Financial Astrology and his Astrology fund, or A-Fund as he called it. I believe the powers behind the curtain on Wall Street panicked when they realized that their secrets could be outed. Thankfully I am not a US Citizen, so the long arm of the SEC does reach into my world. Nevertheless, I do need to be careful about what I say.

Any time I spot a First Trade horoscope with a definite, classic astrology pattern embedded in it, my first instinct is to see what has happened to share price as transiting Sun, Mars, Jupiter and Saturn have passed the corner points of the pattern.

The price chart of NDM shows a peculiar price run-up in 2011 followed by a nasty collapse. Figure 15 illustrates what I have determined from applying the McWhirter method.

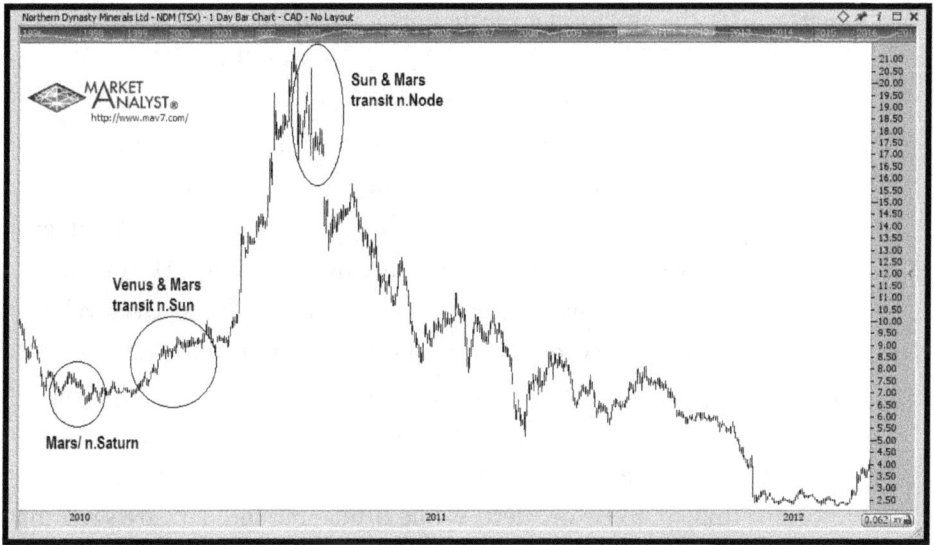

Figure 15 – Northern Dynasty Mining (TSX:NDM) Analysis

Note that Sun and Mars transiting the apex point of the Kite (Node) seem to have triggered the sharp fall in share price.

Moving ahead several years in time, there were more developments with the company.

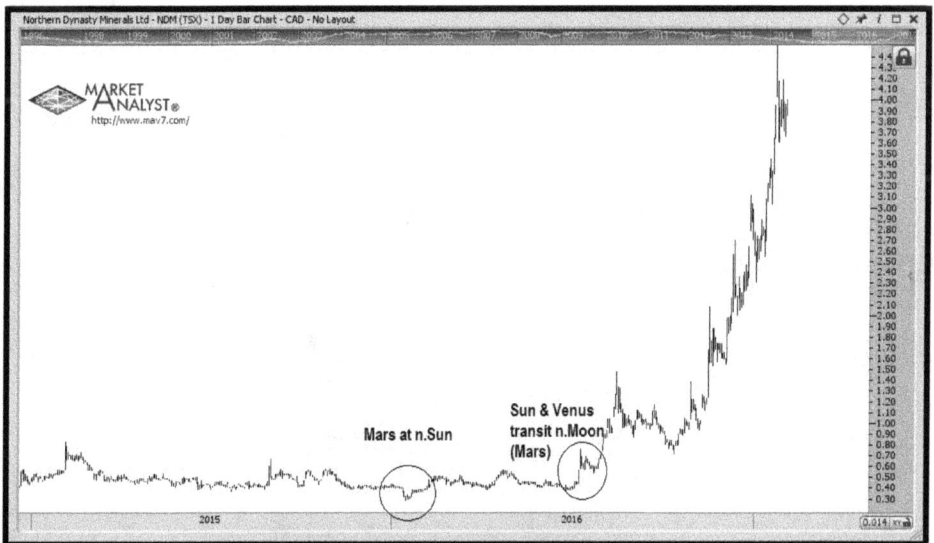

Figure 16 – Northern Dynasty Mining (TSX:NDM) Recovery

In early 2016, the situation appeared grim when the share price hit 30 cents. Quite a tumble from $21 in 2011 to be sure. But, white knight investors came to the rescue and invested heavily in the company. Again transits of the corners of the Kite came into play. As the stock was hitting 30 cents, Mars was passing the natal Sun position. In mid-2016, the share price started to rally with determination, just as Sun and Venus were passing the corner of the Kite home to natal Moon and natal Mars. Share price has had a serious run-up and looks over-valued in the near term. As I complete typing this section, I note that mid to late February, 2017 will see Sun transit the natal Node position. Will this cause a massive correction in the share price or just a levelling off? Or, will the result be a further rise in price? Hard to say, but the important thing is to be on alert. While other shareholders are savoring the recent run-up in price, a student of Astrology, such as yourself, will be alert to possible adverse developments and at the same time open to possible positive developments.

Let's now look at a company that is in the business of supplying fast food outlets and donut shops with roasted coffee beans – Ten Peaks Coffee.

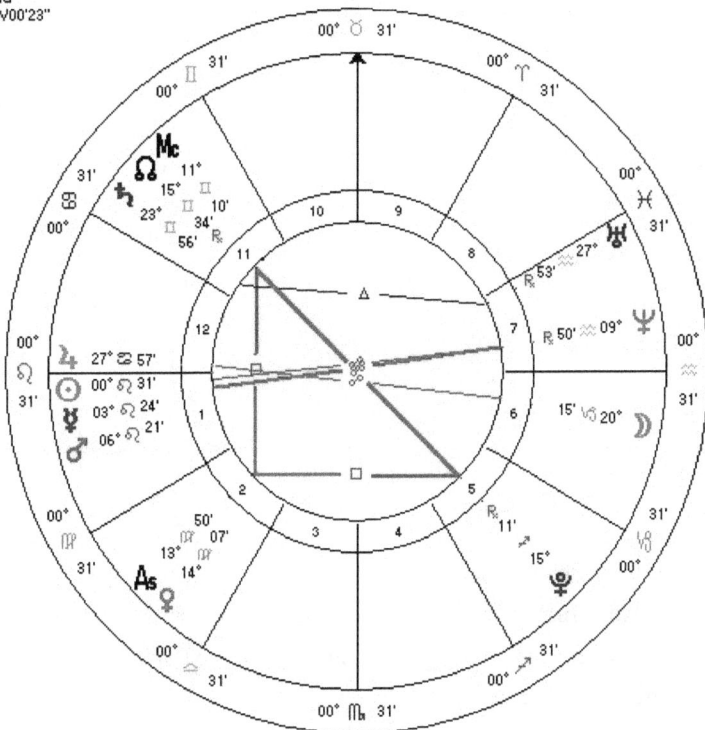

10 Peaks Coffee
Natal Chart
23 Jul 2002, Tue
9·30 am EDT +4·00
Toronto, Canada
40°N42'51" 074°W00'23"
Geocentric
Tropical
Sun on 1st
Mean Node
Parallax Moon

Figure 17 – Ten Peaks Coffee (TSX: TPK) First Trade Horoscope

This is an interesting setup. Sun and Jupiter are conjunct (0 degrees) one another which is a positive energy indicator. Sun is also conjunct Mars which enhances the aggressive energy of Mars. Sun is opposite Neptune which acts to soften any negative energy from Neptune. Neptune and Saturn are 120 degrees apart which serves to ease their negative energies. There is a very obvious T-Square pattern in the horoscope, with the apex at Venus. Normally a T-Square is negative energy, but the Venus apex softens the impact of the T-Square. All in all, this appears to be a good horoscope and this is a company that should survive for a good long time.

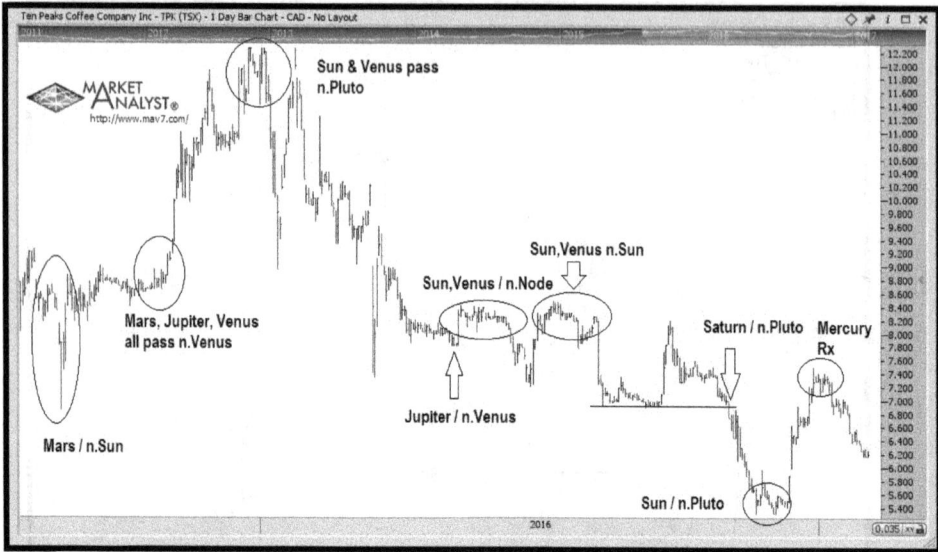

Figure 18 – Ten Peaks Coffee Analysis

The above chart has been overlaid with a number of astrological events. You can see there is a definite correlation to price inflection points. When combined with Wilder Volatility or DMI trend indicators, these astrological events give a trader or investor much added insight into price moves.

For one more example, let's look at the TMX Group that owns and operates the Toronto Stock Exchange in Canada.

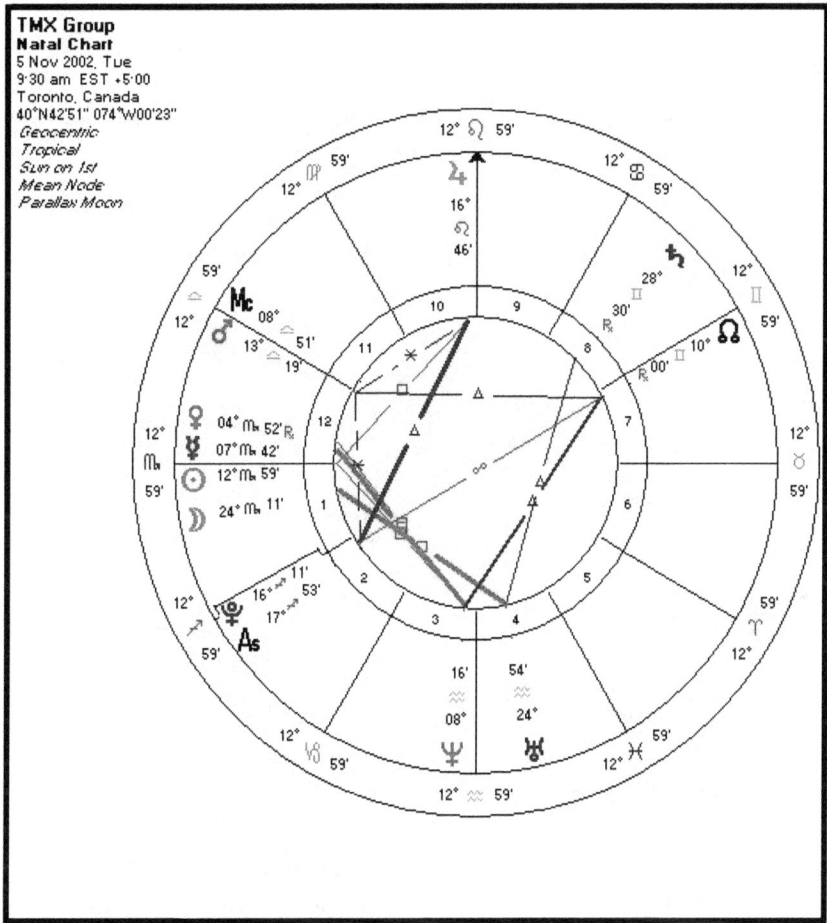

Figure 19 – TMX Group (TSX: X) First Trade Horoscope

This is an interesting set-up for a company in the business of exchange trading and money transfer. Sun is within reach of being conjunct to Mercury and Venus. Expansive planet Jupiter is at the Mid-Heaven which speaks very positively for this Company. Jupiter is 120 degrees to Pluto, so any negative influence from Pluto is softened. Sun/Mercury/Venus are square Neptune and so it's negative energy is softened. Mars is 60 degrees to Jupiter, which eases the aggressive tendencies of Mars. Mars is also 60 degrees to Pluto which is favorable too. All in all, this seems to be a good stock to be involved with. Anytime I see Mercury at a prominent location in a horoscope, I immediately look to see if Mercury Retrograde events play a role in price volatility.

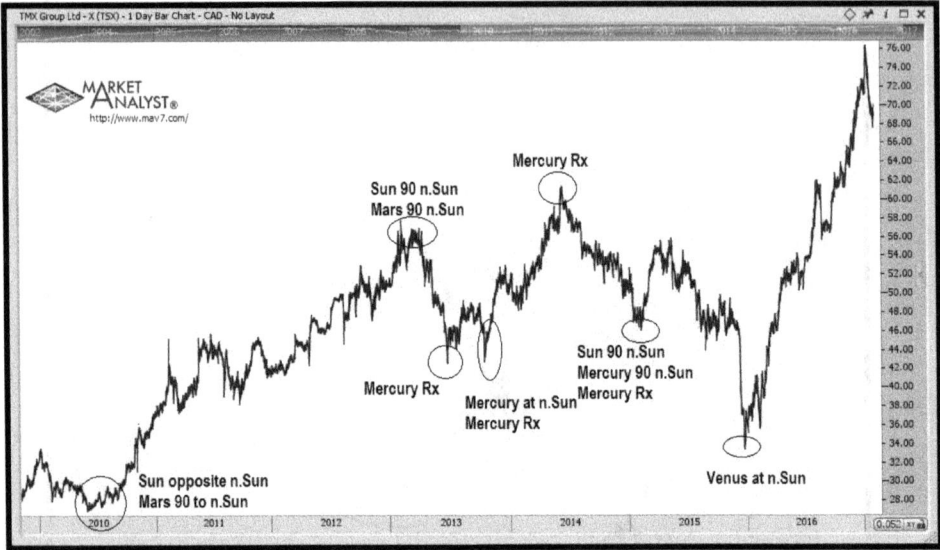

Figure 20 – TMX Group Analysis

The above chart has been overlaid with various astrological events. Just as suggested above, Mercury Retrograde events do play a role in price volatility. In the case of TMX Group, a trader or investor will have significant added insight into price volatility by focusing on these astrological events and combining them with trend indicators.

Commodity Futures

The McWhirter method can be used to gain deeper insight into the price behavior of commodities. If you have never traded commodity futures before, just remember that they are high risk and volatile. Make sure you do not exceed your risk profile.

Crude Oil

As an example, let's look at Crude Oil. West Texas Intermediate Crude Oil futures started trading on a recognized Exchange for the first time on March 30, 1983. A unique alignment of celestial points can be seen in the horoscope in Figure 21. Notice how Mars, North Node, (Saturn/Pluto/Moon) and Neptune conspire to form a rectangle.

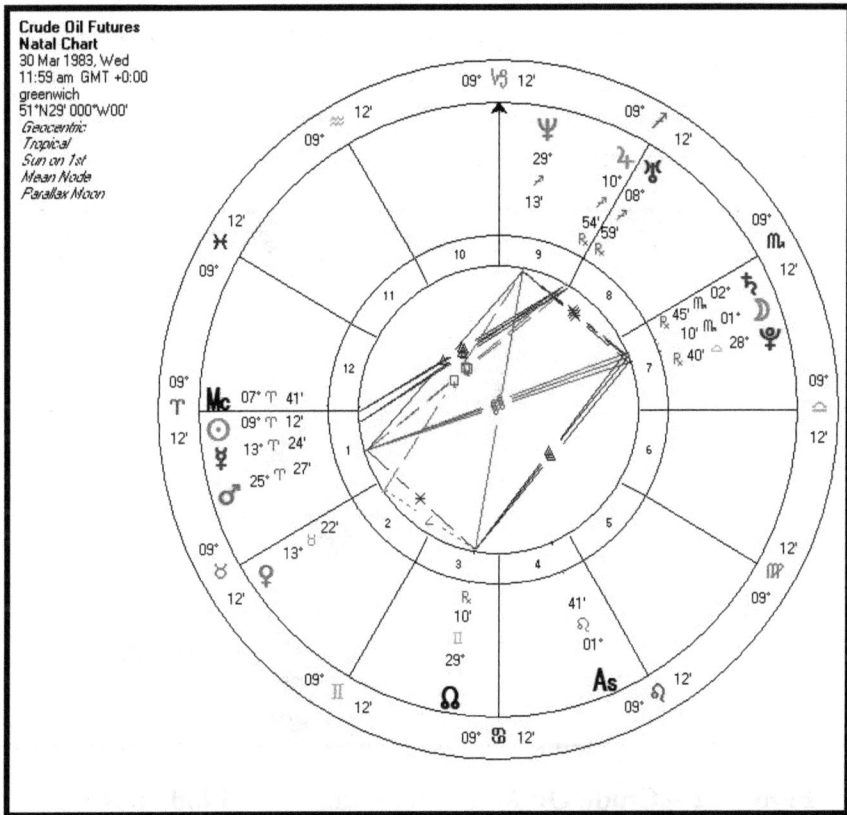

Figure 21 – Crude Oil First Trade Horoscope

The chart in Figure 22 illustrates Oil price action with events of Mars transiting the corner of the rectangle where the Node is situated overlaid. Figure 23 illustrates events of Sun passing the natal Node position. In my opinion, an event of Sun making a 0 degree aspect to the natal Node position is a potent tool to use. Mars passing the Node position is likewise powerful.

In fact, as Figure 22 shows, a transit of Mars past the natal Node location in 2013 came as Oil was hitting $109 a barrel. Price would thereafter struggle to surpass the $109 level and a major sell-off would soon follow.

From this $109 high, price began a sideways movement which led right into the 2014 Sun/Natal Node aspect. This aspect, as shown in Figure 23, marked a major price peak and start of a disastrous trend change on Crude Oil. Another Sun/Node transit in 2015 marked the failure of a brief rally. A transit of Sun past the Node in mid-2016 marked yet another failed rally attempt at the $50 level.

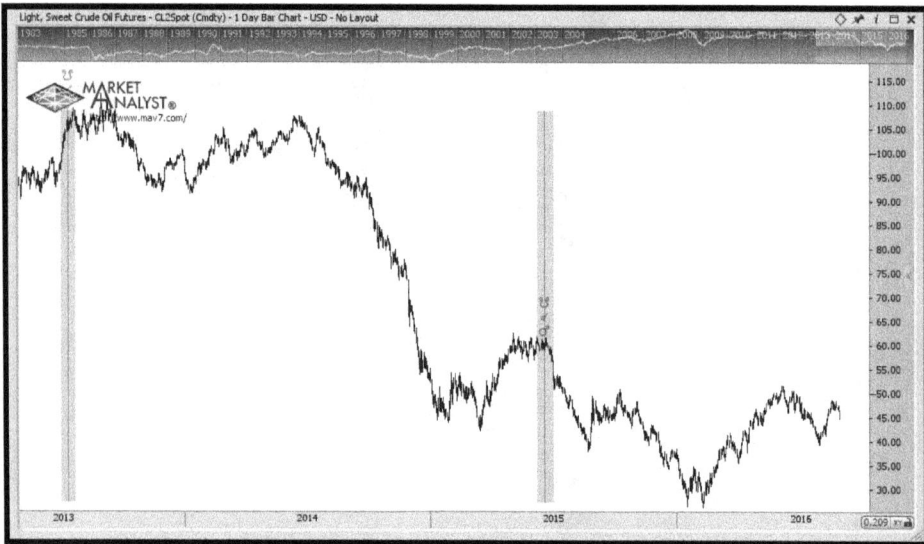

Figure 22 – Crude Oil Mars Transiting natal Node position

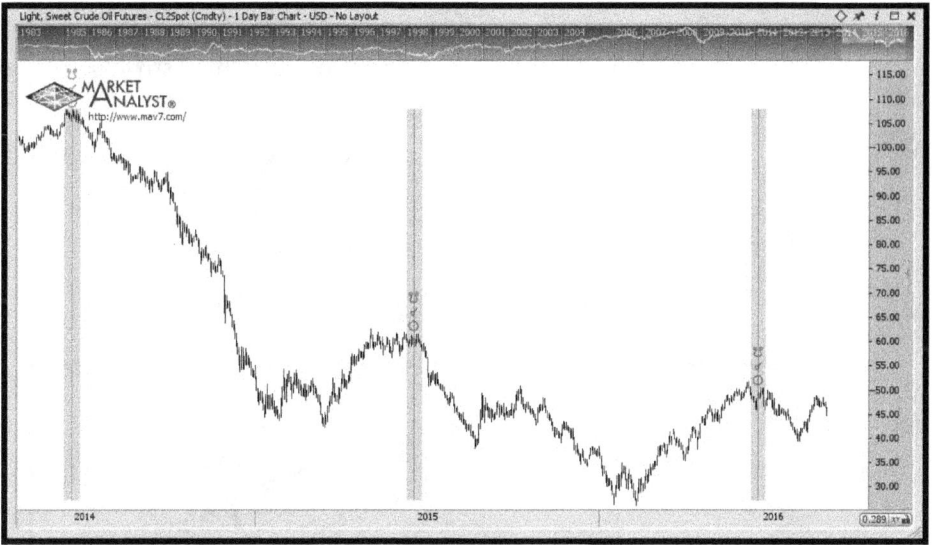

Figure 23 – Crude Oil Sun Transiting natal Node position

Crude Oil is influenced by Mercury Retrograde as well. The Crude Oil price chart in Figure 24 illustrates this effect.

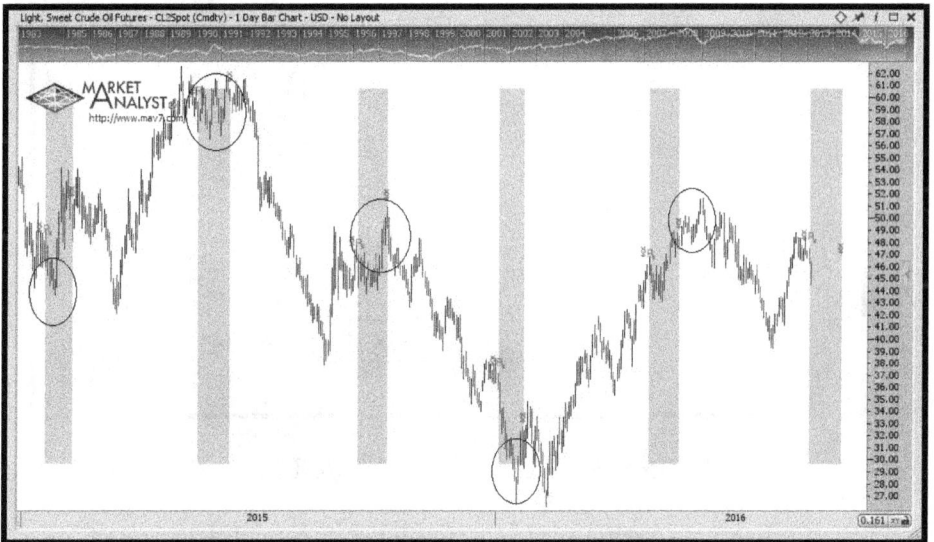

Figure 24 – Crude Oil and Mercury Retrograde

Volatility in Oil futures will directly influence price action of oil companies. If trading Oil futures is not for you, use the Astrology of Crude Oil to assist you with your favorite Oil stocks.

Cotton

W.D. Gann was reportedly an avid trader of Cotton futures.

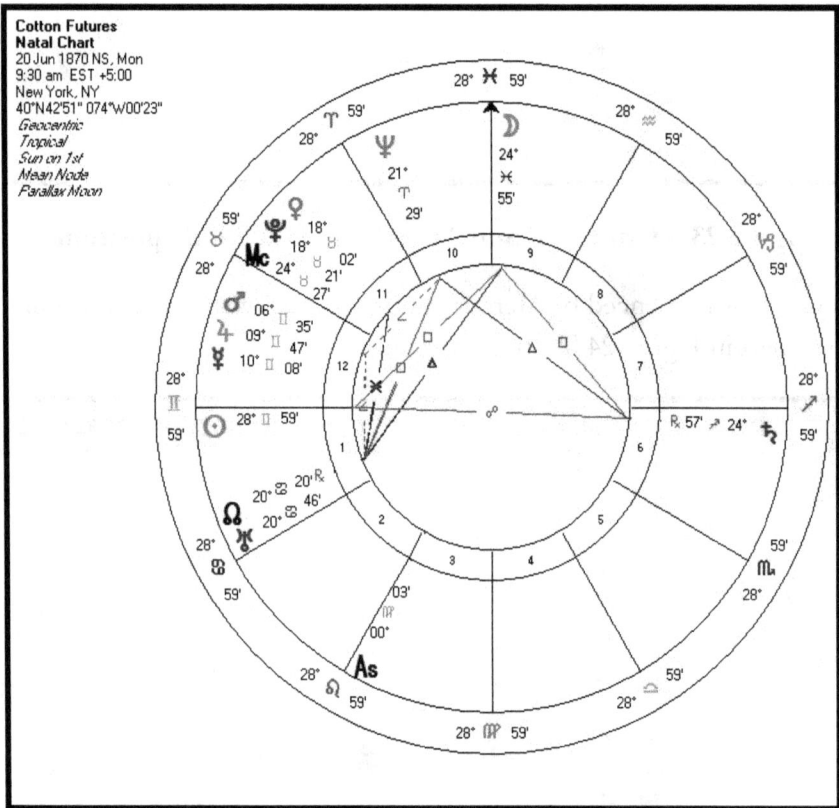

Figure 25 – Cotton First Trade Horoscope

After much painstaking research sifting through back-editions of New York newspapers, I have come to conclude that Cotton futures first started trading on June 20, 1870. The horoscope wheel in Figure 25 illustrates planetary placements at that time. At first glance, I find it peculiar that the Moon is at the same degree and sign location (24

Pisces) as is the Mid-Heaven in the New York Stock Exchange natal horoscope wheel from 1792. Surely this is no accident.

Events of transiting Sun passing 0, 90 or 180 degrees to the natal Sun position are an effective tool for traders to use when navigating the choppy waters of Cotton prices. A suitable chart technical trend indicator is also a must. The Cotton price chart in Figure 26 illustrates further.

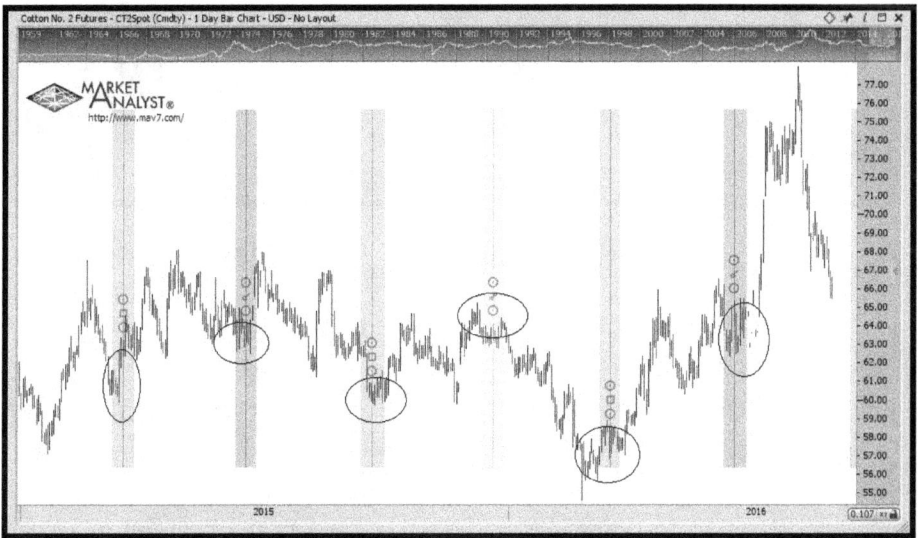

Figure 26 – Cotton and Sun passing natal Sun

One other astrological phenomenon traders may wish to consider as a tool to use is the occurrence of Venus passing by the natal Moon position at 24 Pisces. Not a frequent event, it is nonetheless one to pay attention to. The price chart in Figure 27 illustrates.

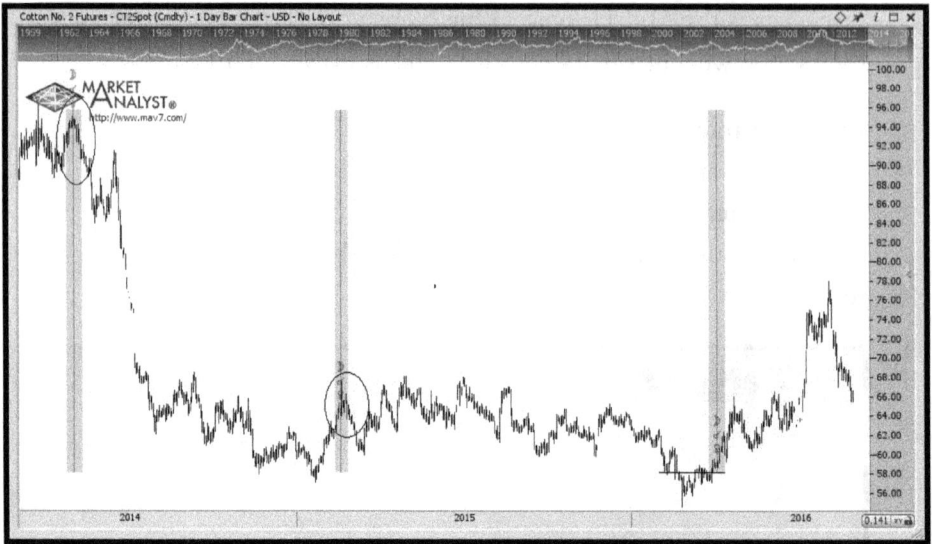

Figure 27 – Cotton and Venus / natal Moon transits

Additional research I have done suggests there may be a once-monthly price inflection as Moon passes 24 Pisces. The chart in Figure 28 illustrates events of Moon passing 24 Pisces. If you are interested in applying this phenomenon to Cotton futures trading, I would suggest studying the hourly charts each month a day or so on either side of the time that Moon is in the process of passing by 24 Pisces. Look for very short term trading opportunities.

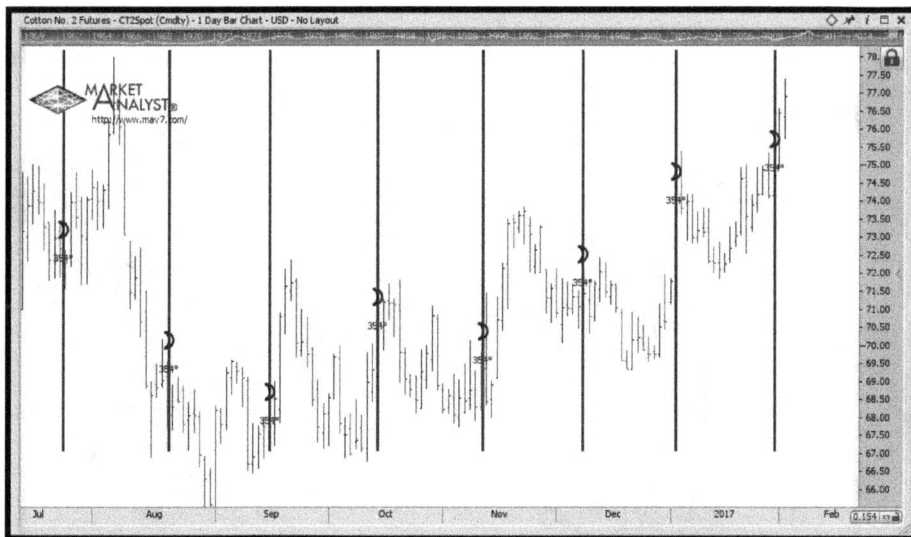

Figure 28 – Cotton and Moon / 24 Pisces

Soybeans

W.D. Gann was also an avid trader of Soybean futures. Soybean futures started trading in Chicago on October 5, 1936. The horoscope in Figure 29 illustrates the planetary placements at that time. What I find intriguing is the location of the Sun. Although not shown here, Sun is exactly 90 degrees to the location of the Sun in the First Trade horoscope for Wheat, Corn and Oats. Surely no accident. As I have previously suggested, the regulatory officials who determine these First Trade dates seem to know more about Astrology than you may think.

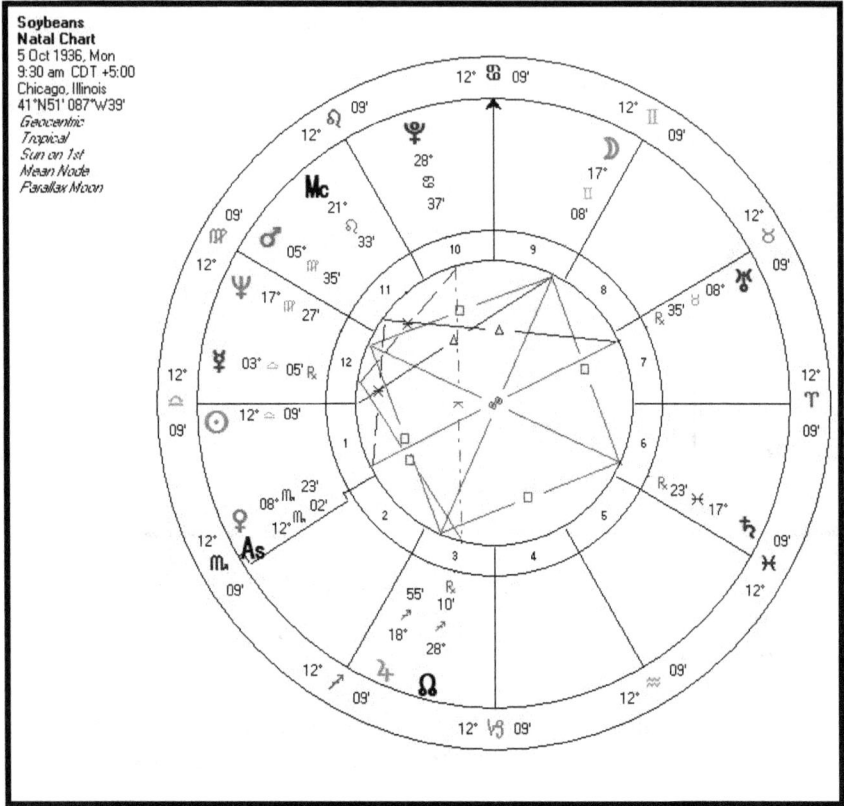

Figure 29 – Soybeans First Trade Horoscope

Events of transiting Sun making 0, 90 and 180 degree aspects to the natal Sun position in the 1936 First Trade horoscope can be used to navigate the volatility of the Soybean market. Figure 30 illustrates the effect of transiting Sun making hard aspects to the natal Sun position. Figure 31 illustrates the effect of Mars making aspects to the natal Sun location.

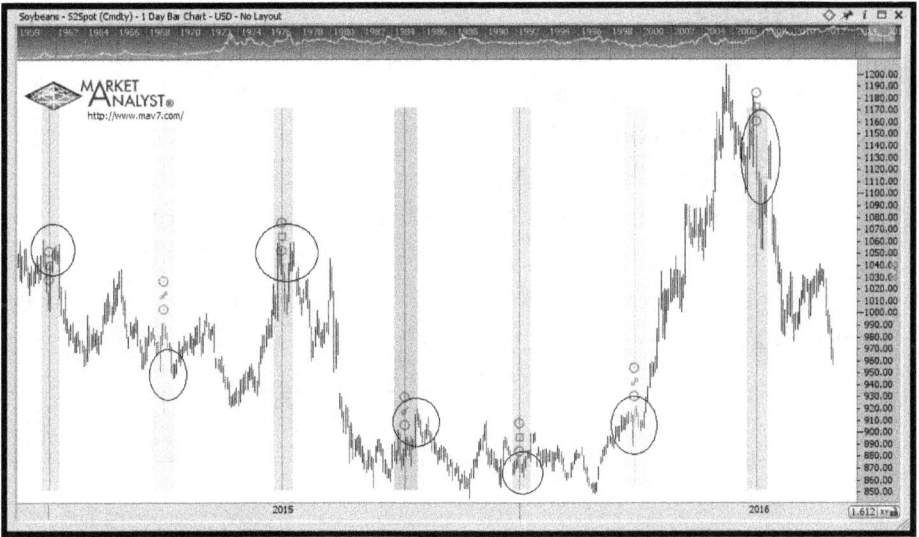

Figure 30 Soybeans and Sun/natal Sun events

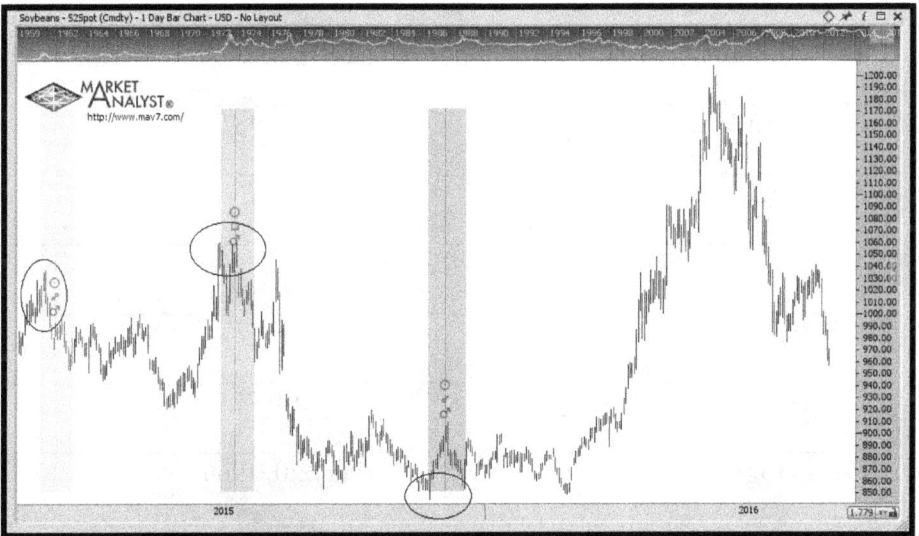

Figure 31 Soybeans and Mars/natal Sun events

As you contemplate these examples, imagine the power you now command. You have insight into an aspect of stocks and commodities that few others have.

Other First Trade Dates

As promised earlier in this section, I said I would provide First Trade dates for various commodities. It has taken me a lot of time and effort to assemble these dates. Sadly, the famous commodity exchanges in New York and Chicago have now ended up in the hands of larger corporations and my inquiries for historical dates and data have variously been met with responses like " that material has been archived away and we have no access to it".

Gold	December 31, 1974
Silver	July 5, 1933
Copper	July 29, 1988
Canadian $, J. Yen, Br. Pound	May 16, 1972
Euro Currency	January 1, 2002
Australian Dollar	January 13, 1987
30 Year Bonds	August 22, 1977
10 Year Treasuries	May 3, 1982
Wheat, Corn, Oats	January 2, 1877
Coffee	March 7, 1882
Lean Hogs	February 20, 1966
Sugar	January 7, 1881
Cocoa	October 2, 1925

Table 1 – Commodity First Trade dates

In your travels, if you come across any First Trade dates for commodities not listed here, please share them with me. It is important that these dates never become lost to the average people if we are to apply Astrology to our trading and investing.

Practical Exercise

Pick a couple of these commodity futures and generate the First Trade charts. Place Sun on the cusp of the First House. As for the time of the chart, pick an early morning hour such as 9:00 am when trading typically would have gotten underway at the Exchange in question. Today, most commodities trade practically around the clock. But, we are not worried about today's hours. The First Trade horoscope will be built around the trading start time decades ago when there was only open-outcry floor trading.

Now, generate a price chart and see if you can spot price inflection points at events involving Sun passing natal Sun and Mars passing natal Sun. Do you see any other correlations?

In my 2017 Almanac I go to great lengths to describe the various correlations I have found on all these commodities.

2. The Albano Method

In addition to McWhirter, I also use the techniques of an Italian astrologer, Giacomo Albano. His one and only financial type book, written in 2012, is aptly titled *"Financial Astrology – How to Predict the Performance of the Financial Markets using Classical Astrology."*

All I can find on the Internet about Mr. Albano is that he was born in 1973, graduated law school in Bologna, Italy and thereafter devoted his time to studying Astrology. A mysterious figure indeed.

The key to understanding Albano's work is, as his book title suggests, classical Astrology. Certainly the McWhirter method relies on classical Astrology, but with Albano it gets a bit deeper and also a bit different.

Albano uses classical Astrology concepts to gain deeper insight into the *general* financial market complex whereas McWhirter focused on the NYSE. Albano does not use these classical concepts to analyze an individual stock or commodity. All he does is try to provide a determination whether the general market will have a positive or negative tenor for a coming period of time.

The Syzygy

Albano's work centers around the 'Syzygy'. By definition, a Syzygy is a pairing of planets or bodies. He uses Sun-Moon pairings of New Moons and Full Moons in his work. Also, he focuses on the New Moon or the Full Moon that occurs immediately prior to Sun transiting into a Cardinal Sign. Cardinal Signs are Aries, Cancer, Libra and Capricorn. We all have plenty of experience with Cardinal Signs. Sun moving into Aries is our Spring Equinox. Sun moving into Cancer marks the Summer Solstice just as Sun moving into Libra marks the Autumn Equinox. Sun moving into Capricorn marks the Winter Solstice which we regard as the start of Winter. As for location, Albano structures his horoscope wheels for Greenwich, England.

The Financial Houses

Albano clearly states that the 2nd, 5th and 8th Houses of the Zodiac wheel are those that pertain to the markets. Each of these Houses is "ruled" by a certain planet. The "ruler" is determined by the Zodiac sign that the House is in. These ruler-ships go way back in history. Study Table 2 or look up any decent website that pertains to Houses and their rulers and you can quickly get a listing of what rules what. For example, if a House division starts in the sign of Aries, Albano says that Mars rules that House because Mars is the "ruler" of Aries. Albano then goes on to consider whether the 2nd, 5th or 8th Houses contain any planets that are in "exaltation" or "exile". Both of these notions are rooted deep in classical Astrology. He then determines what the *'dominus'* of the horoscope wheel is. He further looks to see what planets are *'in their terms'*, which I take to mean *'happy'*. What emerges from this review of a horoscope wheel is a listing of FS planets, where (FS) denotes *Financially Significant*.

Patterns

Once Albano has assessed the planets in the 2nd, 5th and 8th Houses (and the rulers of those Houses), he looks to see if these FS bodies form a discernable geometric pattern. Classical Astrology assigns positive and negative energies to various geometric patterns. If the pattern has positive connotations, Albano then says the markets will generally do well from the Syzygy being analyzed through until the next similar Syzygy. A negative pattern portends a less than favorable outcome. He regards the Point of Thales pattern as positive. Kites and Grand Trines are also highly regarded. Grand Crosses and T-Squares are signs of negative energy. Yods are tending towards the negative. You have already seen a Kite formation in the horoscope of Northern Dynasty Mining in the last section. A T-Square is a right angled triangle with two equal sides. A Grand Cross is two T-Squares put together to form a big square pattern. A Grand Trine is an equilateral triangle where all angles are 120 degrees. A Point of Thales is a right-angled triangle where the three planets in question are at 120 degrees, 180 degrees and 60 degrees from each other. A Yod is a formation involving three planets where angular separations are 150, 150 and 60 degrees. Look back at Figure 29 – the First Trade horoscope for Soybeans. You can see a Point of Thales made of Mars, Uranus, Venus. You can see a T-Square made of Neptune, Saturn, Jupiter. You can see a Grand Cross made of Neptune, Moon, Saturn, Jupiter.

Ruling Planets

Here is a Table of what astrologers deem to be the ruling planets for the various Zodaic signs.

Zodiac Sign	Ruling Planet
Aries	Mars
Taurus	Venus
Gemini	Mercury
Cancer	Moon
Leo	Sun
Virgo	Mercury
Libra	Venus
Scorpio	Mars and Pluto
Sagittarius	Jupiter
Capricorn	Saturn
Aquarius	Saturn and Uranus
Pisces	Neptune and Jupiter

Table 2 Ruling Planets

Exaltations and Exile

Here is a Table of additional data pertinent to the Albano methodology.

Zodiac Sign	Exaltation	Exile
Aries	Sun 18-19 degrees Aries	Saturn
Taurus	Moon 2-3 degrees Taurus	
Gemini		
Cancer	Jupiter 14-15 degrees Cancer	Mars
Leo		
Virgo	Mercury 14-15 degrees Virgo	Venus
Libra	Saturn 20-21 degrees Libra	Sun
Scorpio		Moon
Sagittarius		
Capricorn	Mars 27-28 degrees Capricorn	Jupiter
Aquarius		
Pisces	Venus 26-27 degrees Pisces	Mercury

Table 3 Exaltation and Exile

Terms

Aries	Jupiter 0-6	Venus 6-14	Mercury 14-21	Mars 21-26	Saturn 26-20
Taurus	Venus 0-8	Mercury 8-15	Jupiter 15-22	Saturn 22-26	Mars 26-20
Gemini	Mercury 0-7	Jupiter 7-14	Venus 14-21	Saturn 21-25	Mars 25-30
Cancer	Mars 0-6	Jupiter 6-13	Mercury 13-20	Venus 20-27	Saturn 27-30
Leo	Saturn 0-6	Mercury 6-13	Venus 13-19	Jupiter 19-25	Mars 25-30
Virgo	Mercury 0-6	Venus 7-13	Jupiter 13-18	Saturn 18-24	Mars 24-30
Libra	Saturn 0-6	Venus 6-11	Jupiter 11-19	Mercury 19-24	Mars 24-30
Scorpio	Mars 0-6	Jupiter 6-14	Venus 14-21	Mercury 21-27	Saturn 27-30
Sagittarius	Jupiter 0-8	Venus 8-14	Mercury 14-19	Saturn 19-25	Mars 25-30
Capricorn	Venus 0-6	Mercury 6-12	Jupiter 12-19	Mars 19-25	Saturn 25-30
Aquarius	Saturn 0-6	Mercury 6-12	Venus 12-20	Jupiter 20-25	Mars 25-30
Pisces	Venus 0-8	Jupiter 8-14	Mercury 14-20	Mars 20-26	Saturn 26-30

Table 4 Terms

Lilith

As was pointed out in Course 1, the Moon revolves around the Earth in a somewhat elliptical pattern. Think of an elliptical pattern as that of an egg or a slightly elongated circle. Mathematically, an ellipse will have two focal points. In the case of the Moon, one of the elliptical focal points is planet Earth. The second focal point is a purely mathematical construct and to astrologers this focal point is called *Lilith*. A very close approximation to Lilith is the time when Moon is at its Apogee (farthest point) from the Earth every 29.5 day lunar cycle. If the Moon at its Apogee point happens to be conjunct to a financially significant planet (FS), Albano urges caution. Your Ephemeris tables or your software program will help you find Moon Apogee dates.

The Albano method is challenging – even more so than the McWhirter method. The best way to grasp its power and elegance is to study some examples. The key to Albano, is to keep an open mind and not get too bogged down in all the subtle nuances of classical Astrology.

June 2016 Syzygy

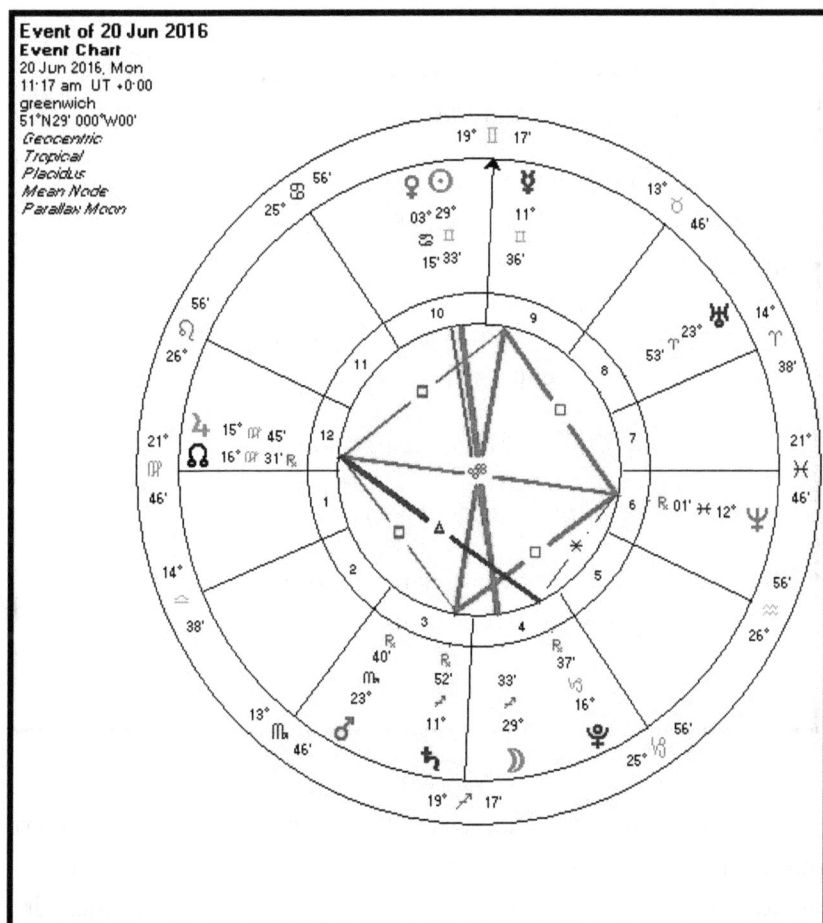

Figure 32 June 20, 2016 Syzygy

The Full Moon of June 20, 2016 was the lunar event immediately prior to the Sun's ingress into cardinal point Cancer. Hence, Albano calls it a Syzygy. Figure 32 illustrates the planetary placements.

The following observations can be taken from this horoscope.

2nd House: Libra ruled by Venus

5th House: Capricorn ruled by Saturn which (although not present in the 5th) is Retrograde and weakened.

8th House: Aries ruled by Mars. Mars is Retrograde which weakens it. Uranus also in the 8th.

The Syzygy in this horoscope wheel is the Full Moon of June 20 which occurred mere days before Sun moved into Cardinal Sign Cancer.

Venus is conjunct the Sun so is the "dominus" of the horoscope wheel. Venus is also (FS).

No planets are exalted. None are in exile.

Jupiter is in its "terms" at 15 of Virgo.

Sun, Moon, Venus, Saturn, Uranus are thus deemed to be Financially Significant (FS) in this horoscope wheel.

The square pattern (Grand Cross) evident in the horoscope is made of Jupiter, Saturn, Neptune and Mercury. Normally a Grand Cross is deemed to be a powerful occurrence. But, of the planets that make it up, only Saturn is financially significant, but Saturn is weakened in Retrograde. Weakened Saturn in this pattern somewhat offsets Jupiter which is *in its terms*. Venus, which is the (FS) planet that happens to be conjunct (0 degrees) to Sun, is the *"dominus"* of this horoscope. Venus is a positive planet, so from this Syzygy until the next one, the market complex should generally be positive, but not overwhelmingly so.

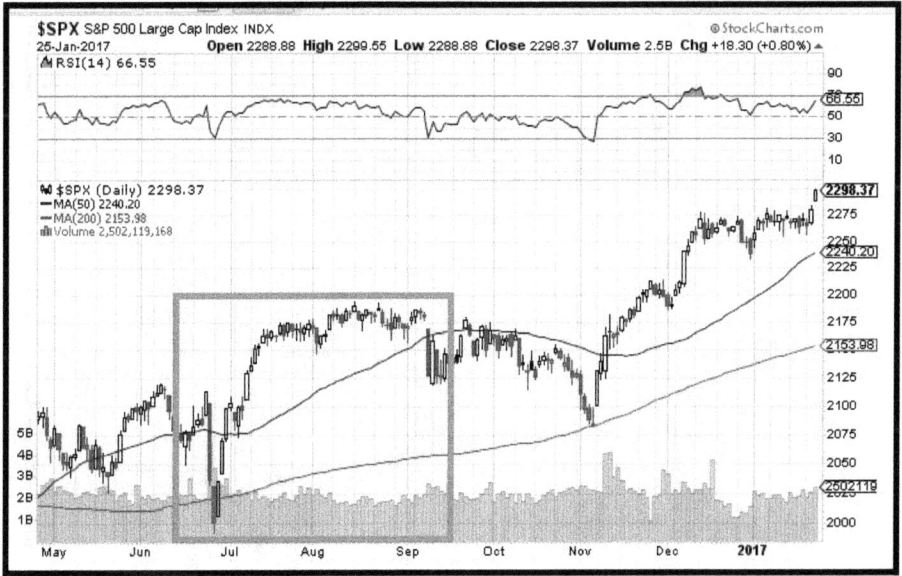

Figure 33 S&P 500 after the June 2016 Syzygy

As Figure 33 shows, the S&P 500 generally moved higher following this Syzygy event. But, there was volatility along the way. Hence the importance of watching the short term trend carefully.

September 2016 Syzygy

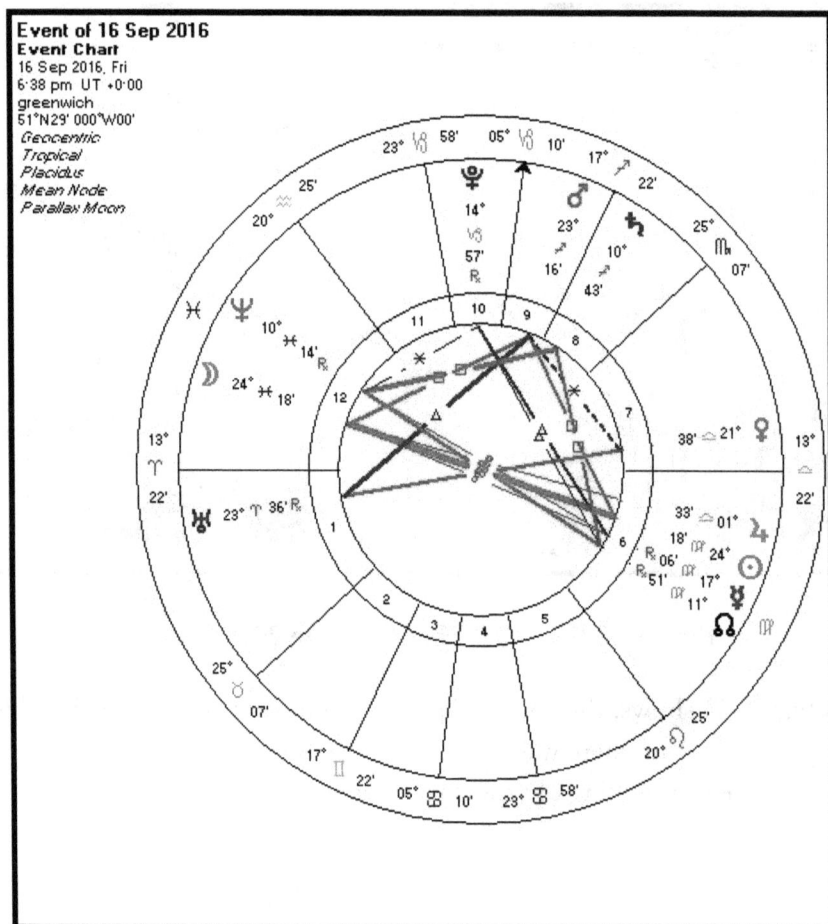

Figure 34 September 16, 2016 Syzygy

The Full Moon of September 16, 2016 was the lunar event immediately prior to the Sun's ingress into cardinal point Libra. Hence, Albano calls it a Syzygy. Figure 34 illustrates the planetary placements.

The following observations can be taken from this horoscope.

2nd House: Taurus ruled by Venus

5th House: Cancer ruled by Moon.

8th House: Scorpio ruled by Mars and Pluto. Saturn is also present in the 8th.

The Syzygy in this horoscope wheel is the Full Moon of September 16 which occurred several days before Sun moved into Cardinal Sign Libra.

Mars forms a T-Square with Sun and Moon.

Mercury is exalted in Virgo and rules Virgo, but this is offset by it being Retrograde. Mercury is also "*combust*". A planet is combust (debilitated) if it is within 8 degrees of Sun in its own sign.

No planet in its "terms", no planets in exile.

Sun, Moon, Venus, Mars, Pluto and Saturn are deemed to be Financially Significant (FS) in this horoscope wheel.

In this horoscope, I see two Points of Thales and two T-Squares. Venus and Uranus are 180 degrees opposite each other. Uranus in turn is 120 degrees to Mars. Mars is 60 degrees to Venus. This pattern is the first Point of Thales and it is modestly positive because Uranus is not (FS) and this weakens the Point of Thales pattern. Neptune, Pluto and Mercury make the second Point of Thales. Mercury is combust and Neptune is not (FS) so the pattern is weak. The Sun-Moon-Mars T-square points of Mars aggressive energies. The other T-square of

Neptune, Node, Saturn has only Saturn being (FS) which weakens the pattern. The Albano method then is suggesting only a modestly positive period from the September 2016 Syzygy to the next Syzygy.

Figure 35 S&P 500 after the September 2016 Syzygy

As the above chart shows, the S&P 500 did on balance exhibit modest positive behavior. But, the Albano method did not predict the sharp drawdown into the November Presidential election. Nor did it predict the sharp re-bound immediately after.

December 2016 Syzygy

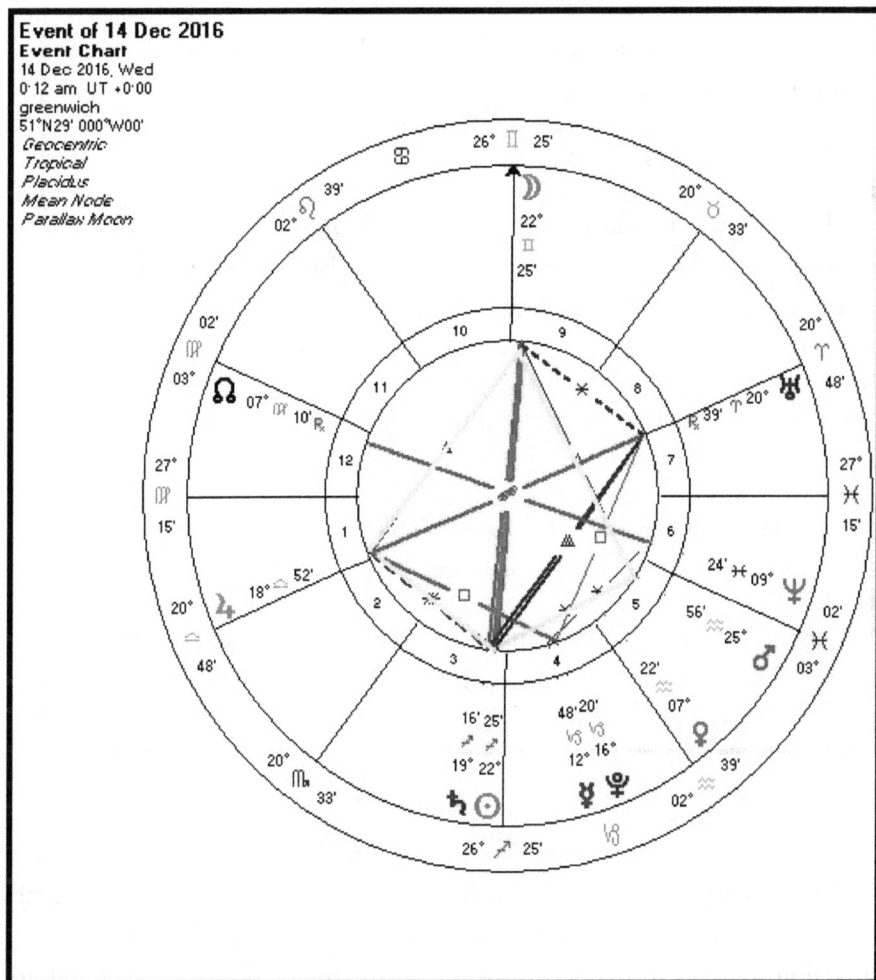

Figure 36 December 14, 2016 Syzygy

The Full Moon of December 14, 2016 was the lunar event immediately prior to the Sun's ingress into cardinal point Capricorn. Hence, Albano calls it a Syzygy. Figure 36 illustrates the planetary placements.

2nd House: Libra ruled by Venus

5th House: Aquarius ruled by Uranus and Saturn. Venus and Mars also in the 5th.

8th House: Aries ruled by Mars.

The Syzygy in this horoscope wheel is the Full Moon of December 14 which occurred several days before Sun moved into Cardinal Sign Capricorn.

Saturn is conjunct Sun, and is the "dominus" of the horoscope wheel. Saturn is in its "terms" in Sagittarius which softens its heavy-weight reputation.

Note carefully the pattern I have overlaid in yellow. This is a "Kite" and it is powerfully positive.

Venus, Sun, Moon, Mars, Jupiter are deemed to be Financially Significant (FS) in this horoscope wheel.

Markets have responded very well since the December Syzygy. In fact in late January, the DOW tested the area above 20,000 for the first time ever. The mainstream media is at a loss as to how markets can be reacting so favorably to a President that the media abhorred so much in the campaign. Perhaps the media should study Astrology. This "Kite" formation says the markets were destined to rise higher, regardless of who was picked to occupy the White House.

March 2017 Syzygy

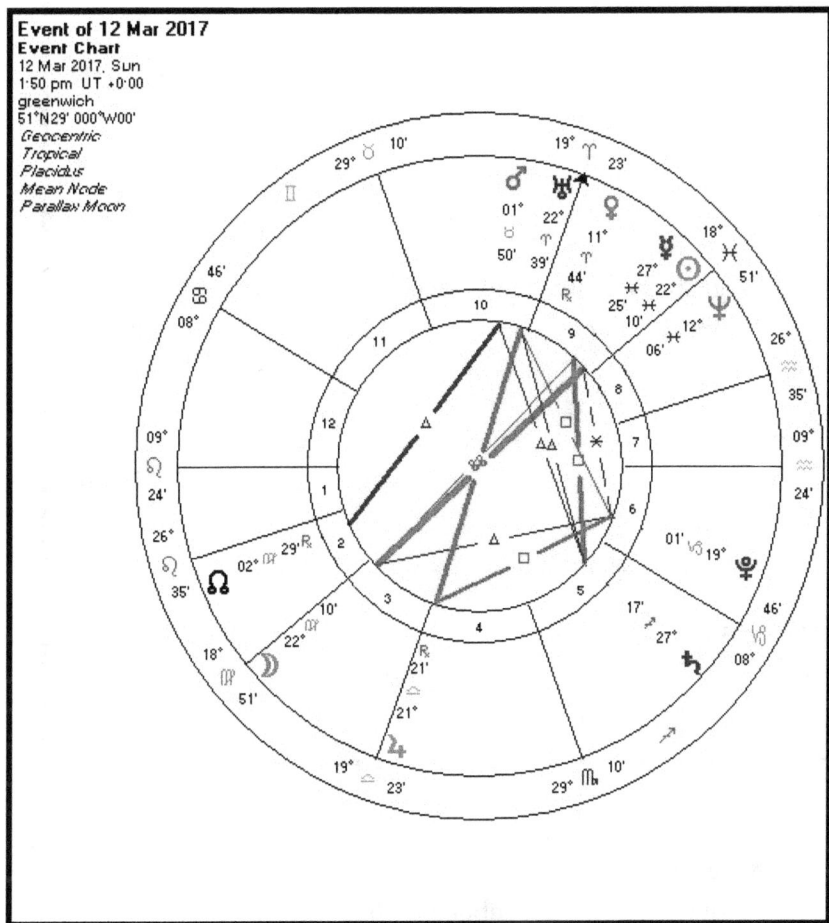

Figure 37 March 12, 2017 Syzygy

The Full Moon of March 12, 2017 was the lunar event immediately prior to the Sun's ingress into cardinal point Aries. Hence, Albano calls it a Syzygy. Figure 37 illustrates the planetary placements.

I see a Moon-Pluto-Sun Point of Thales and a Jupiter-Uranus-Pluto T-Square.

2nd House: Leo ruled by Sun

5th House: Scorpio ruled by Mars. Saturn is also in the 5th. Mars and Saturn are 120 degrees apart.

8th House: Aquarius ruled by Uranus and Saturn, which are a favorable 120 degrees apart. Neptune is also in the 8th.

The Syzygy in this horoscope wheel is the Full Moon of March 12, 2017 which will occur several days before Sun moves into Cardinal Sign Aries.

Mercury is conjunct Sun, and is the "dominus" of the horoscope wheel. Sun(Mercury), Moon and Pluto form a Point of Thales. But Moon and Pluto are not (FS). Jupiter, Uranus, Pluto form a T-Square, but only Uranus is (FS).

Saturn, Sun, Mars, Uranus, Neptune are deemed to be Financially Significant (FS) in this horoscope wheel.

This Syzygy is not as powerful as the one in December, 2016. In fact, it is quite weak. Remember too that Mercury will be Retrograde for a while starting early April. Venus will also be Retrograde March 4-April 14.

Hence, the powerful positive uplift to the markets is likely to ease off from March 2017 through June 2017.

June 2017 Syzygy

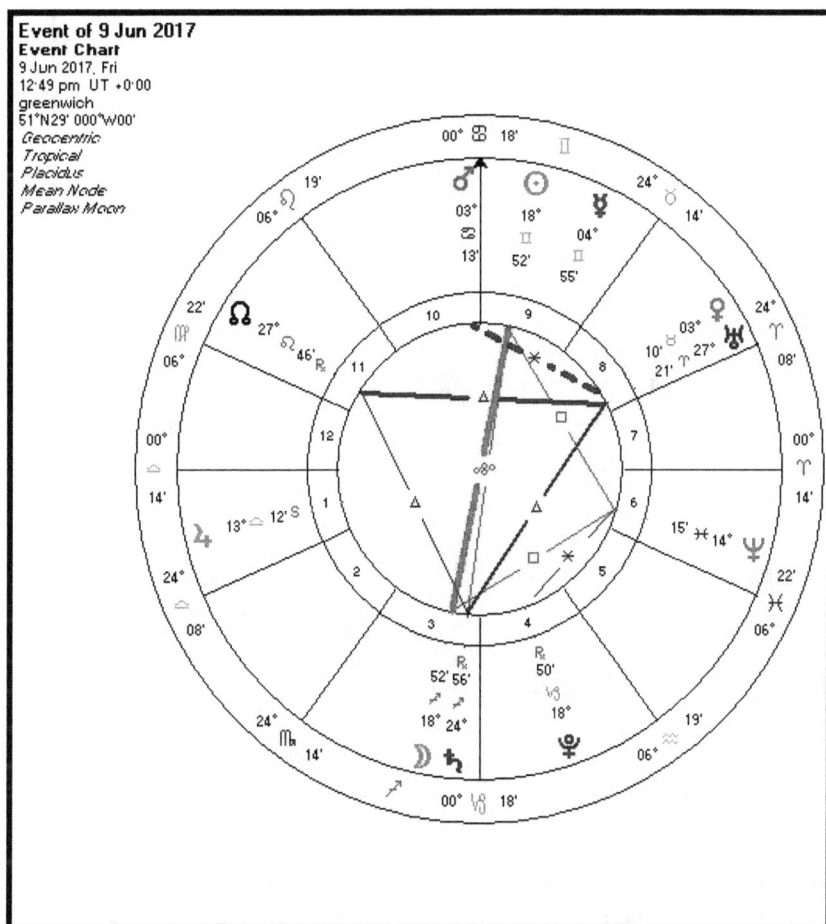

Figure 38 June 9, 2017 Syzygy

The Full Moon of June 9, 2017 was the lunar event immediately prior to the Sun's ingress into cardinal point Cancer. Hence, Albano calls it a Syzygy. Figure 38 illustrates the planetary placements. I see a Grand Trine of Node, Saturn and Venus(Uranus). I see a Sun-Moon-Neptune T-Square.

2nd House: Libra ruled by Venus

5th House: Aquarius ruled by Uranus and Saturn. Saturn is in its terms in Sagittarius.

8th House: Aries ruled by Mars. Venus and Uranus are in the 8th. Mars is in exile in Cancer so is weakened.

The Syzygy in this horoscope wheel is the Full Moon of June 9, 2017 which will occur several days before Sun moves into Cardinal Sign Cancer.

Venus is in its terms in Taurus and is the "dominus" of the horoscope wheel. Sun, Moon and Neptune form a T-Square which is not really relevant as none are (FS). What is relevant is the Grand Trine involving Saturn and Venus(Uranus).

Venus, Uranus, Saturn, Mars, Uranus are deemed to be Financially Significant (FS) in this horoscope wheel.

Note carefully that this date comes 1 day after a Moon Apogee date (Lilith) and Moon is conjunct evil Saturn.

This Syzygy is relatively better than the previous Syzygy. But the Lilith point conjunct Saturn may have something to say to the contrary. Hence, look for a relative positive tone to the market complex from June, 2017 through September 2017, but beware of sudden volatility.

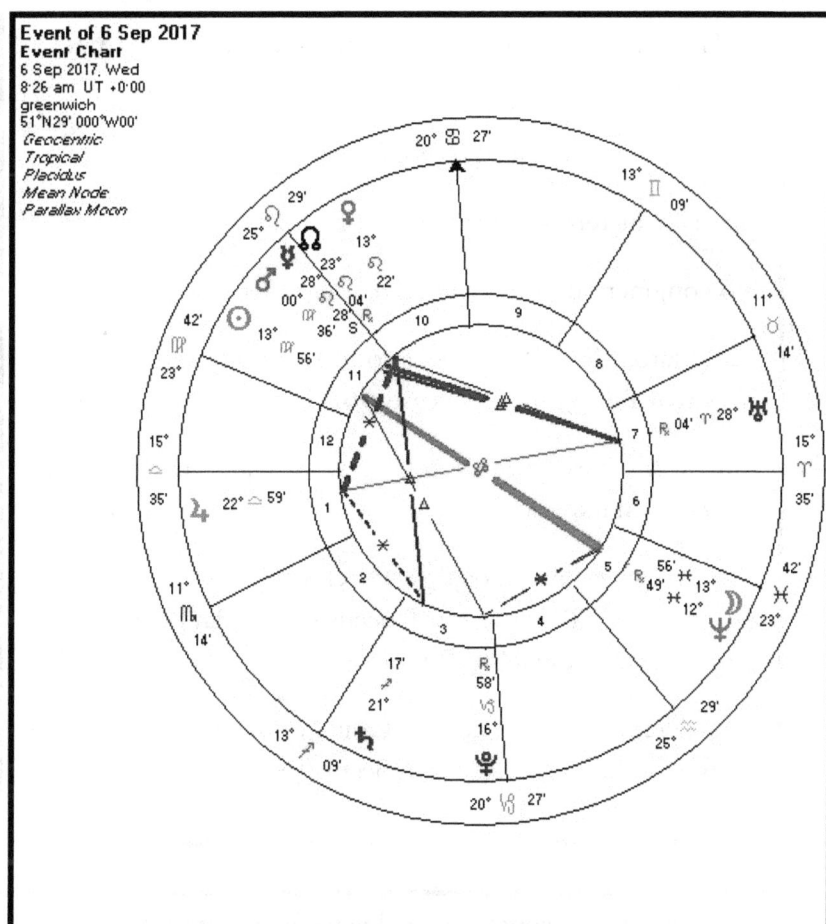

Figure 39 September 6, 2017 Syzygy

The Full Moon of September 6, 2017 was the lunar event immediately prior to the Sun's ingress into cardinal point Libra. Hence, Albano calls it a Syzygy. Figure 39 illustrates the planetary placements. I see two Point of Thales patterns in this horoscope.

2nd House: Scorpio ruled by Mars and Pluto. Mars has just emerged from exile in Cancer.

5th House: Aquarius ruled by Uranus and Saturn. Neptune and Moon also in the 5th.

8th House: Taurus ruled by Venus.

Venus in its terms in Leo, Saturn in its terms in Sagittarius.

No conjunction to Sun in Virgo. Mercury rules Virgo.

Sun, Pluto, Moon(Neptune) also form a Point of Thales. The apex is at Pluto, which suggests volatility.

Jupiter, Mercury (Mars) and Uranus form a Point of Thales. Mercury (Mars) is at the apex suggesting volatility.

The Syzygy in this horoscope wheel is the Full Moon of September 6, 2017 which will occur several days before Sun moves into Cardinal Sign Libra.

Mars, Pluto, Uranus, Saturn, Moon, Neptune, Venus are deemed to be Financially Significant (FS) in this horoscope wheel.

This set-up is reasonably firm due to the Point of Thales patterns. Mercury seems important in this set-up, being the ruler of the Sun's sign and being part of a Thales pattern. Bear in mind that this Syzygy comes two days after a Mercury Retrograde wraps up. Watch for a trend change to occur, most likely to the upside. Watch for lots of volatility.

I would like to circle back and further use Albano's work to hone in closer and see if it portended the low point that coincided with the US Election.

Let's start with the **New Moon Syzygy of September 1, 2016.**

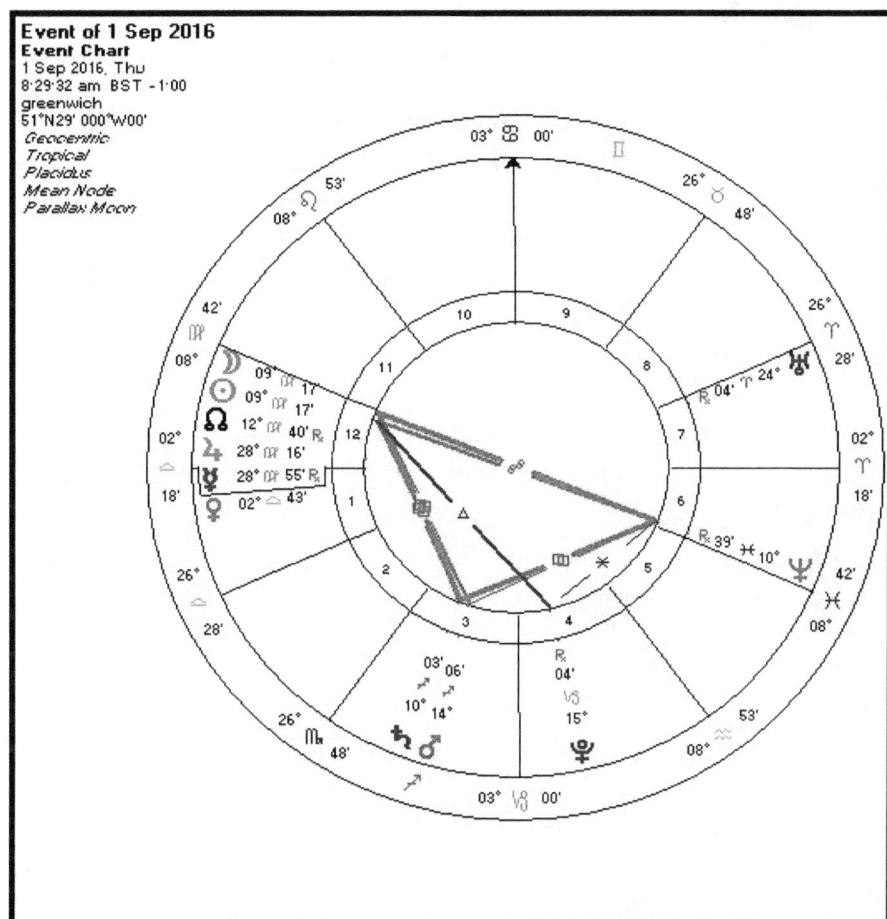

Event of 1 Sep 2016
Event Chart
1 Sep 2016, Thu
8·29·32 am BST -1·00
greenwich
51°N29' 000°W00'
Geocentric
Tropical
Placidus
Mean Node
Parallax Moon

Figure 40 September 1, 2016 Syzygy

2nd House: Libra ruled by Venus.

5th House: Aquarius ruled by Uranus and Saturn.

8th House: Aries ruled by Mars.

Sun, Neptune, Pluto form a Point of Thales. But, it is weakened as none are (FS).

The Syzygy in this horoscope wheel is the New Moon of September 1, 2016.

Mars, Uranus, Saturn, Venus are deemed to be Financially Significant (FS) in this horoscope wheel.

There is a T-square pattern evident in the chart made up of Sun, Neptune, Saturn (Mars). Neptune is not (FS). Only Saturn/Mars are (FS) and they are at the apex of this pattern. So, this pattern, although negative, is weakened somewhat. The following chart shows a weaker market, but only slightly so.

Figure 41 S&P 500 after the September Syzygy

Let's now examine the **New Moon Syzygy of October 1, 2016**

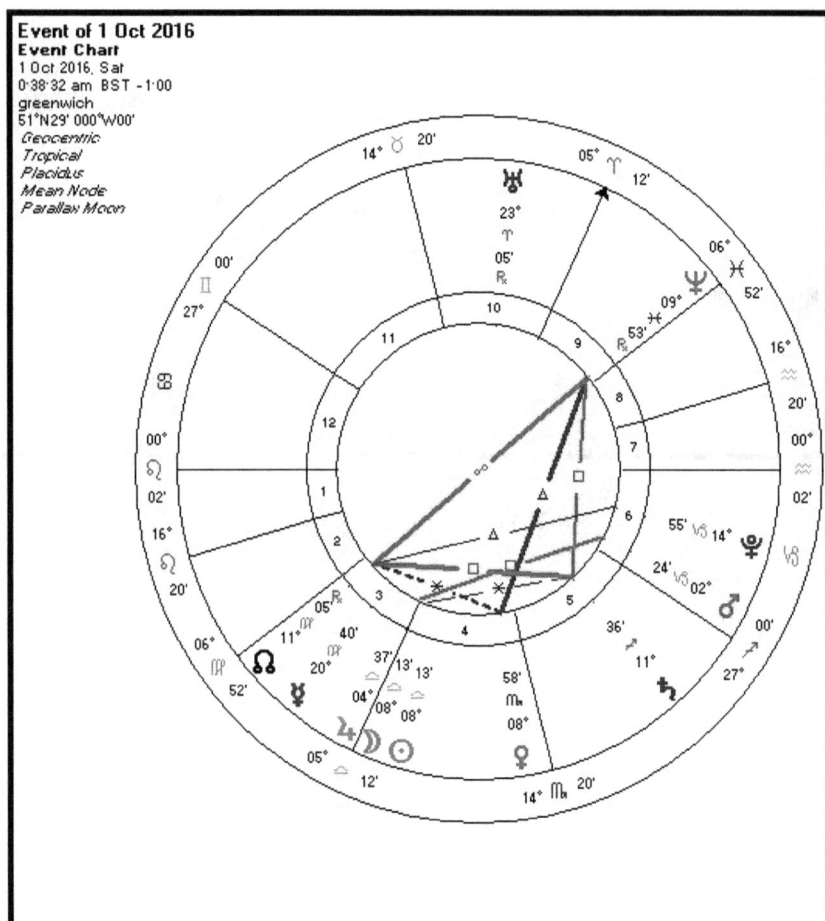

Figure 42 October 1, 2016 Syzygy

2nd House: Leo ruled by Sun.

5th House: Scorpio ruled by Mars and Pluto.

8th House: Aquarius ruled by Uranus and Saturn.

Node, Neptune, Venus form a Point of Thales. But, it is weakened as none are (FS). Jupiter is the 'dominus' but not (FS). A weak indictor for sure.

The Syzygy in this horoscope wheel is the New Moon of October 1, 2016.

Mars, Pluto, Uranus, Saturn, Sun are deemed to be Financially Significant (FS) in this horoscope wheel.

Mars is square to the New Moon syzygy. There is a T-Square formation made of Neptune, Node and Saturn. Only Saturn, at the apex of the T-Square, is (FS). So, yes a T-Square, but a weakened one. As this chart shows, this weak pattern did cause a drop in the markets, but this pattern gave no hints as to the magnitude of the drop.

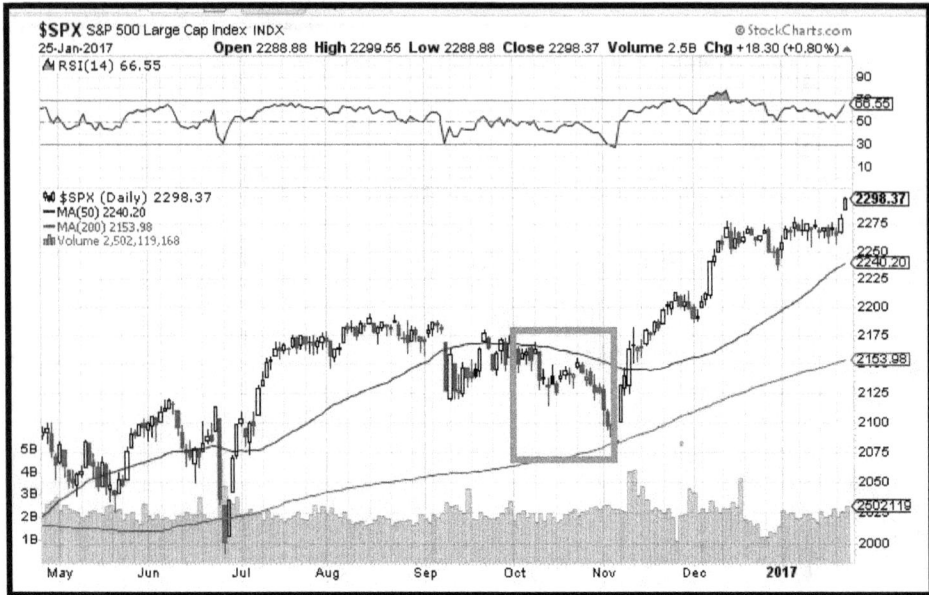

Figure 43 S&P 500 after the October 2016 Syzygy

Let's now examine the **New Moon Syzygy of October 30, 2016**

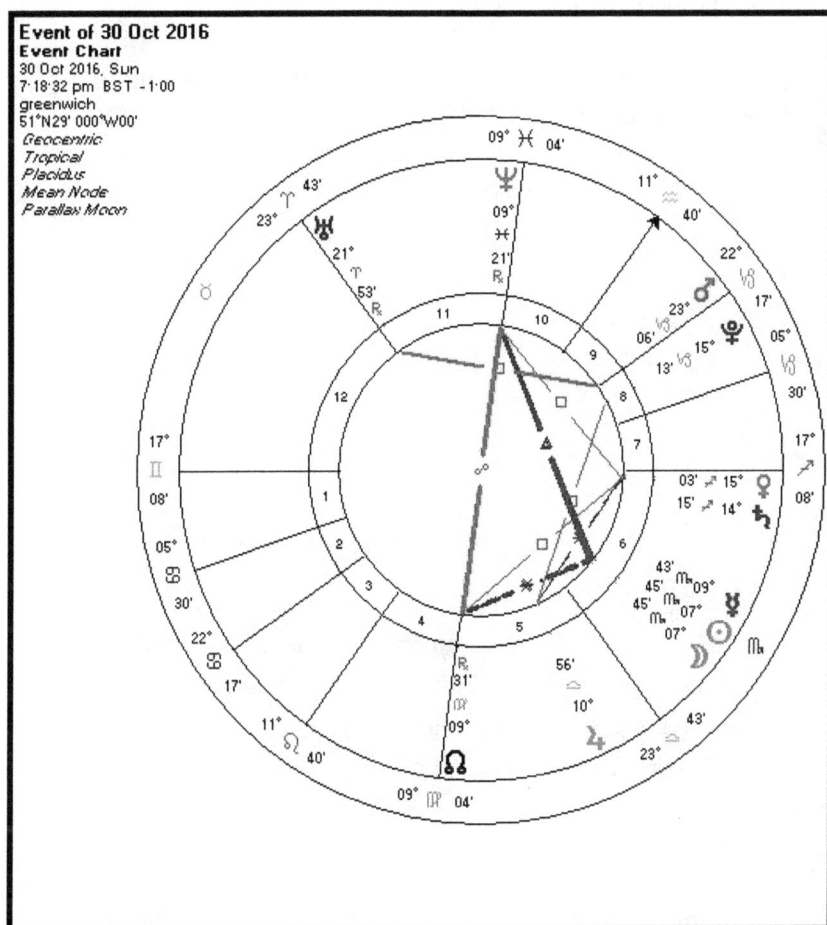

Figure 44 October 30, 2016 Syzygy

2nd House: Cancer ruled by Moon.

5th House: Virgo ruled by Mercury. Mercury is conjunct Sun so is the 'dominus'.

8th House: Capricorn ruled by Saturn.

Node, Neptune, Mercury/Sun form a Point of Thales.

The Syzygy in this horoscope wheel is the New Moon of October 30, 2016.

Sun, Moon, Mercury, Saturn are deemed to be Financially Significant (FS) in this horoscope wheel.

There is a Point of Thales made up of Neptune, Node and Sun/Moon. This is powerful given that the Sun/Moon apex point is the Syzygy. There is also a T-square of Neptune, Node, Venus/Saturn. But it is weakened as only Saturn is (FS). Venus is in "its terms" at 15 Sagittarius which weakens the pattern more.

The positive and powerful Point of Thales makes this Syzygy more robust than the last one. This Syzygy event comes 1 day ahead of a Moon Apogee (Lilith). Note although this Syzygy is more robust than the last one, Lilith still may weigh into the equation.

Figure 45 S&P 500 after the October Syzygy

As the chart shows, positive and powerful are apt descriptors for what happened. But, note that Lilith did appear to have impacted the market in the days immediately after the Moon Apogee event. Then the positive aspects of this Syzygy took over and pushed the market up.

So, all in all, the Albano method is complex and deeply rooted in classical Astrology. Don't be upset if you get overwhelmed when trying to use it. The key is practice, practice, practice. I have 5 years of this stuff under my belt and I still find Albano's work to be mind-warpingly complicated. But, I keep using it because I think it has a lot of merit. If I could offer one more bit of advice, instead of using Albano to look at every Syzygy, maybe just start by looking just at the four main annual events that immediately precede the Sun moving into Cardinal signs during the year. This will give you a general feel for what a coming calendar quarter will look and feel like.

To re-cap, the basic steps are as follows:

1. Generate the horoscope wheel for the Syzygy event immediately prior to the date when Sun transits into a Cardinal sign. This may turn out to be a New Moon or a Full Moon event.

2. Examine the 2nd, 5th and 8th Houses. Make a list of the planets in those Houses as well as a list of the ruler(s) of those Houses. These are your (FS) planets.

3. Look next for chart patterns like T-Squares, Points of Thales, Grand Crosses, Grand Trines, Kites. Are these patterns made up of any (FS) planets? Based on the planets that comprise these patterns, how would you describe the pattern? Strong, Weak, modestly strong, modestly weak? Keep it simple.

4. Are any planets in Exaltation or Exile? Are any planets in Terms?

5. Is there a planet conjunct to Sun? Is it (FS)?

6. Now move ahead in time and generate the horoscope for the next date that occurs immediately prior to Sun moving into the next cardinal sign.

7. Repeat this analysis and determine if this Syzygy is weaker or stronger than the previous Syzygy. This will give valuable hints as to the tenor of the markets in the coming months.

8. To hone in closer on market action, generate horoscope charts for all monthly New Moons and Full Moons. Analyze as above. This will give you a more in-depth prognosis.

3. The Weston Model

Cosine Motion

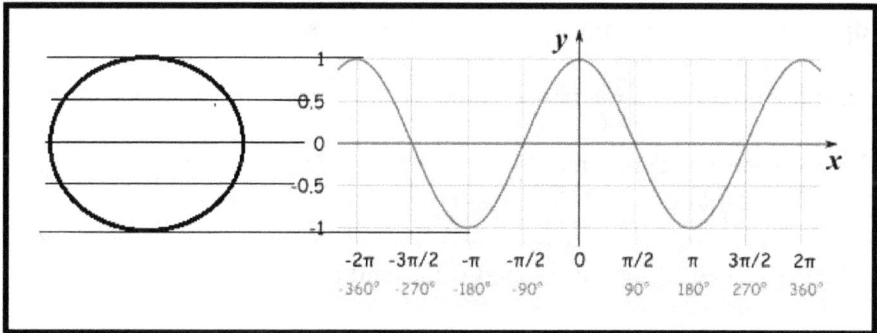

Figure 46 Circular Motion and the Cosine curve

This final section of Course 2 is going to take you deep into the realm of cosine curves. This material is not easy to grasp and you may end up having to talk to someone who majored in mathematics in college to fully get your head wrapped around everything. Some time ago, late at night, whilst scouring the Internet looking for old Astrology manuscripts for sale, I came upon a white paper written in 1921 by another mysterious person going by the name of Professor Weston from Washington, D.C. I paid $50 for this product, and I am thrilled that I did. Never in my research travels to various libraries have I come across this name. I cannot find any other publications by him, although I understand there might be two more out there somewhere. Who exactly he was, I will likely never know. Another one of those figures who emerged to write his ideas down and then vanished into the ether.

So, let's start with some basics. As Figure 46 shows, circular motion around the circumference of a circle can be translated into a cosine curve. This is not a new phenomenon. The mathematics relating circular motion to sinusoidal or cosine curves dates back to the ancient Babylonians. Our formal knowledge of this branch of mathematics reached a pinnacle with the work of Newton, Euler and others in the 1600s and 1700s.

What if we had circles all of varying sizes being translated into sinusoidal or cosine curves? What if we combined the sinusoidal or cosine outputs and smoothed the outputs into one curve? Such was the question posed by French mathematician Joseph Fourier. His work opened the door to the notion of the Fourier series.

Simply put, a Fourier series would take the form:

Y = cosine (fundamental frequency 1) + cosine (fundamental frequency 2) +......

The general equation can consist of several terms if need be.

Plotting Y on a graph where Y (from the above general equation) is the vertical axis and the horizontal axis is Time would yield a strange looking wavy curve. A trader or investor would look closely at this plot and focus on the highs and lows of the plot. Figure 47 illustrates a typical plot that extends over 700 months.

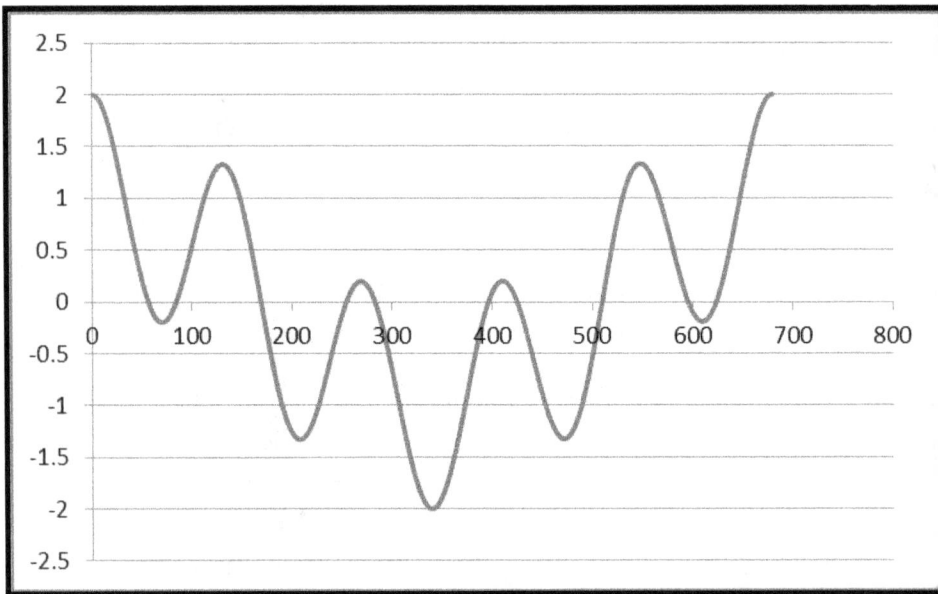

Figure 47 Typical Plot of a Fourier Series

Have you seen plots that look somewhat like this before? I think you may have. In Course 1, I presented plots of planetary declination. The various planets all exhibit varying degrees of declination over time, but the plots are all curvilinear. As another example, if you have ever seen an oscilloscope that measures electrical wave patterns, you have seen plots like this. The connection between Fourier series plots and Nature is deeper than we think. And this speaks to the root of Weston's work. He posited that the price plot of a stock, commodity or index was really just a combination (a Fourier series)of sinusoidal or cosine equations.

In the above general equation, where do we get the fundamental frequencies? The answer is we get them from studying a long term, monthly price chart. On that chart we look for major, significant price highs.

Let's suppose we found a chart where there were two major highs and they occurred **34 years** apart. Let's further suppose that within this long interval there were four other major highs. So, in total over 34 years we would count **6 highs**. Next we would look for a span of time shorter than 34 years where there were two major bottoms. Let's suppose in this example we noted two major lows and they occurred **27 years** apart.

Now, we can engineer some mathematics.

34 years divided by 6 = 5.66 years = 67.92 months.

27 years divided by 5.66 = 4.77 = 5 in round figures.

Therefore, 5 times 5.66 = 28.3 = 339.6 months.

360 divided by 339.6 = 1.06 degrees = 0.0185 radians (recall there are 2 pi radians in a circle).

360 divided by 67.92 = 5.30 degrees = 0.0925 radians.

Our general equation then becomes:

Y = cosine (A) + cosine (B); where A=0.0185 and B=0.0925

$Y = \text{cosine } (0.0185 \text{ radians}) + \text{cosine } (0.0925 \text{ radians})$

Next we will set up a simple spreadsheet on a computer that takes the form as follows:

X	Y
1	Cosine (A) + Cosine (B)
2	Cosine (2A) + Cosine (2B)
3	Cosine (3A) + Cosine (3B)
4	Cosine (4A) + Cosine (4B)
5	Cosine (5A) + Cosine (5B)
And so on…	And so on…

We will structure this spreadsheet so that it extends for many hundreds of months.

We will then plot the output using the X-Y plot graphing function in our spreadsheet program. The result will look like the following graph.

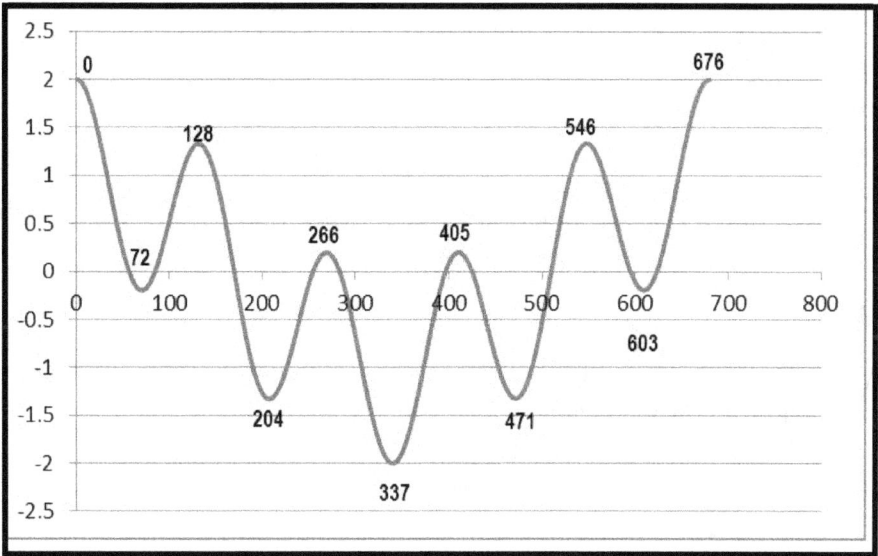

We will next use our plot to see when we can reasonably expect the next price inflection point. In the above sample plot, there should be price inflections 72, 128, 204, 266 etc… months from the zero starting point. The zero start point will either be the first significant high point or the first major low point on our monthly price chart.

This sample plot, by the way, is of Coffee futures and the zero point is the major low in March 1975. I detailed this example in one of my bi-weekly astrology E-Alert newsletters in late 2016.

I have found that the key to using Weston's work is to keep it simple. The markets do not operate on pin-point precision. When you identify an inflection point on your plotted output, you can count ahead in time to see if it aligned to an actual price inflection, but do so with a +/- 1 month time frame. Weston's model should also be used in combination with other astrological events.

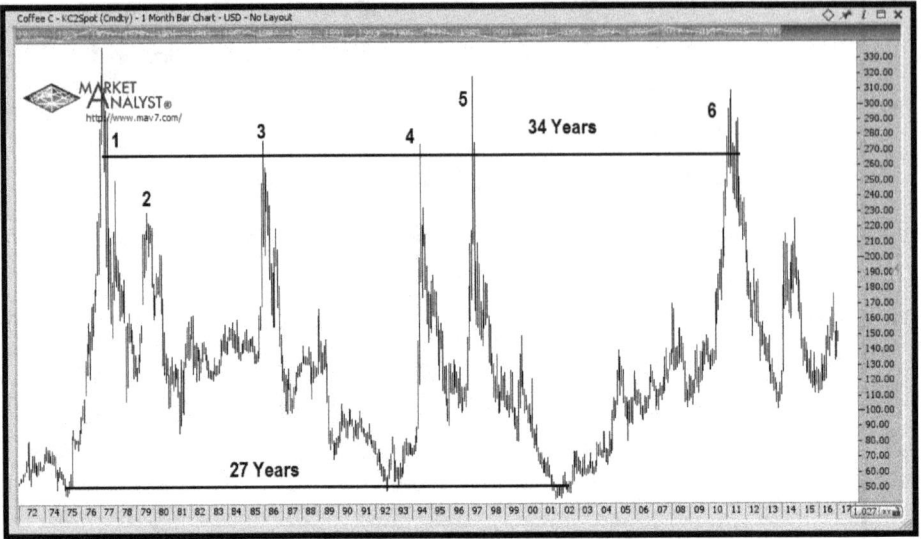

Figure 48 Long Term Monthly Coffee Futures

Is your brain about to short circuit due to mathematical confusion? Don't feel bad. Weston's work is not exactly easy. With practice, it will start to become more manageable.

Let's look at a couple examples, starting with Gold futures.

The following is a long term monthly chart of Gold futures dating back to 1975.

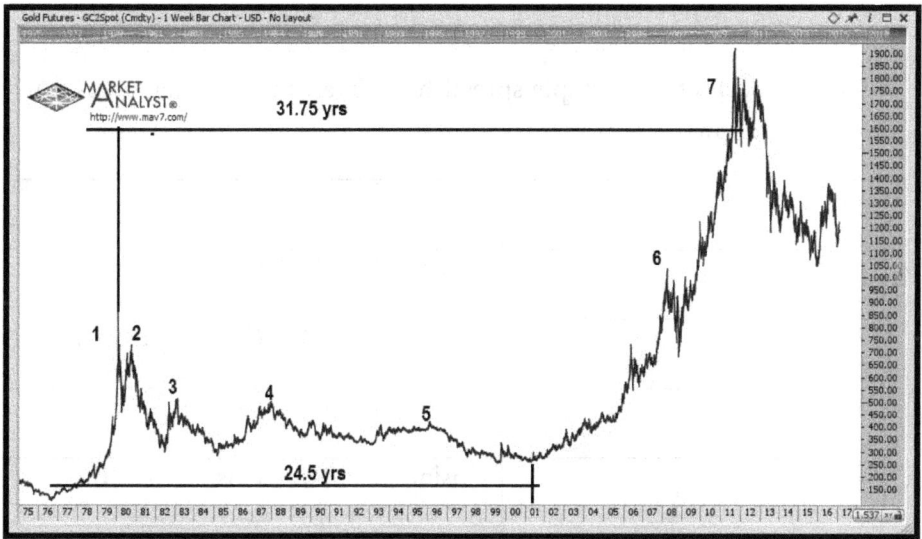

Figure 49 Long Term Monthly Gold Futures

In Figure 49 we can see there were two major highs and they occurred **31.75 years** apart. In this long interval there were five other major highs. So, in total over 31.75 years we would count **7 highs**. Next we look for a span of time shorter than 31.75 years where there were two major bottoms. In this chart we note two major lows and they occurred **24.5 years** apart.

Now, we can engineer some mathematics.

31.75 years divided by 7 = 4.53 years = 54.42 months.

24.5 years divided by 4.53 = 5.40 = 5 in round figures.

Therefore, 5 times 4.53 = 22.65 = 271.8 months.

360 divided by 271.8 = 1.324 degrees = 0.0231radians (recall there are 2 pi radians in a circle).

360 divided by 54.42 = 6.615 degrees = 0.1154 radians.

Our general equation then becomes:

$Y = \cosine (A) + \cosine (B)$; where A=0.0231 and B=0.1154

$Y = \text{cosine } (0.0231 \text{ radians}) + \text{cosine } (0.1154 \text{ radians})$

Next we will set up a simple spreadsheet on a computer that takes the form as follows:

X	Y
1	Cosine (0.0231) + Cosine (0.1154)
2	Cosine (0.0462) + Cosine (0.2309)
3	Cosine (0.0693) + Cosine (0.3463)
4	Cosine (0.0924) + Cosine (0.4618)
5	Cosine (0.1155) + Cosine (0.5772)
And so on… for 700 rows	And so on…for 700 rows

The resulting X-Y plot looks like this:

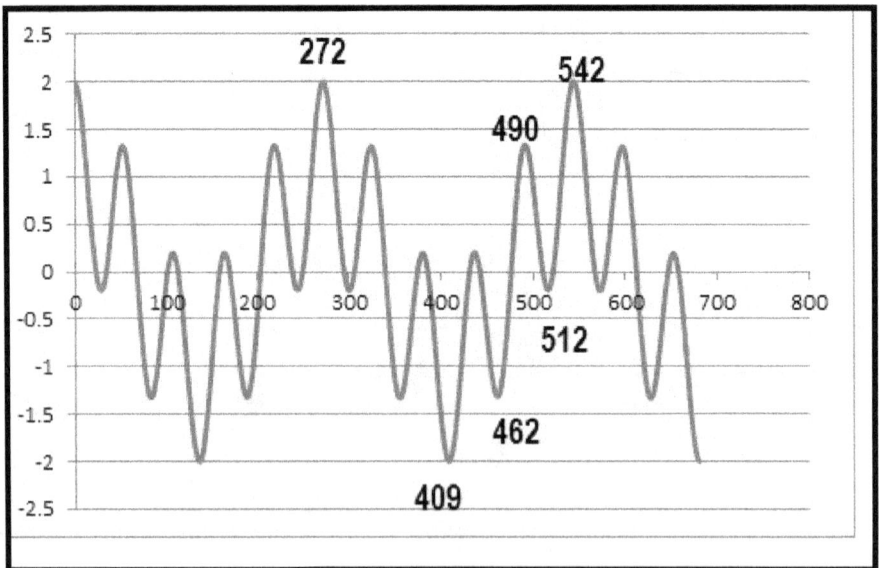

Figure 50 X-Y Plot of Gold Cosine Functions

Using a zero start point of the August 1976 low, I have checked several of these plotted intervals and they do indeed align reasonably well with inflection highs and lows on the historical monthly Gold chart. Note further that the data point at 490 months from the zero point equates to June 2017 – so as I write this manuscript, we are drawing close to what should be another price inflection point on Gold. Will it be a high or a low? Following the price trend indicators in combination with other Astrology techniques will help us make that call. In the June 2017 time frame, both Mars and Sun will transit 180 degrees past the 1974 Gold First Trade natal Sun.

Let's take a look at another case, this time Crude Oil.

The following is a long term monthly chart of WTI Crude futures dating back to the 1980s.

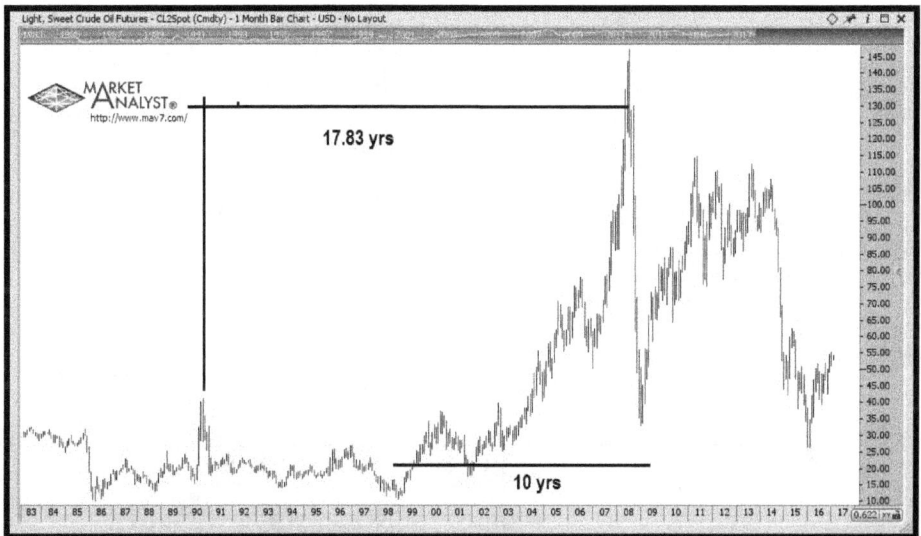

Figure 51 Long Term Monthly WTI Oil Futures

In Figure 51 we can see there were two major highs and they occurred **17.83 years** apart. In this long interval there were three other major highs. So, in total over 17.83 years we would count **5 highs**. Next we look for a span of time shorter than 17.83 years where there were two major bottoms. In this chart we note two major lows and they occurred **10 years** apart.

Now, we can engineer some mathematics.

17.83 years divided by 5 = 3.566 years = 42.79 months.

10 years divided by 3.566 = 2.804 = 3 in round figures.

Therefore, 3 times 3.566 = 10.69 = 128.37 months.

360 divided by 128.37 = 2.804 degrees = 0.0489 radians (recall there are 2 pi radians in a circle).

360 divided by 42.79 = 8.4131 degrees = 0.1468 radians.

Our general equation then becomes:

Y = cosine (A) + cosine (B); where A=0.0489 and B=0.1468

Y = cosine (0.0489 radians) + cosine (0.1468 radians)

Next we will set up a simple spreadsheet on a computer that takes the form as follows:

X	Y
1	Cosine (0.0489) + Cosine (0.1468)
2	Cosine (0.0978) + Cosine (0.2936)
3	Cosine (0.1468) + Cosine (0.4405)
4	Cosine (0.1957) + Cosine (0.5873)
5	Cosine (0.2446) + Cosine (0.7341)
And so on… for 700 rows	And so on…for 700 rows

The resulting X-Y plot looks like this:

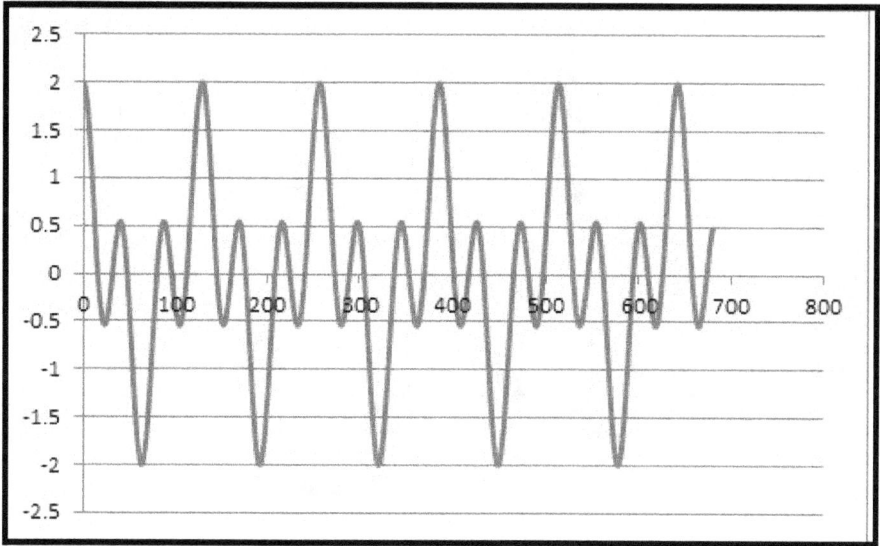

Figure 52 X-Y Plot of Oil Cosine Functions

Using a zero start point of the March 1986 low, I have checked several of these plotted intervals and they do indeed align reasonably well with inflection highs and lows on the historical monthly Oil chart. Note further that the data point at 216 months from the 1990 (Desert Storm War) lands at the July 2008 highs. From the 1998 low, data point 197 says to be alert for an inflection. In fact one came – in early 2016 as Crude collapsed to under $30.

Let's take one more example, this time Cocoa futures.

The following is a long term monthly chart of Cocoa futures dating back to 1959.

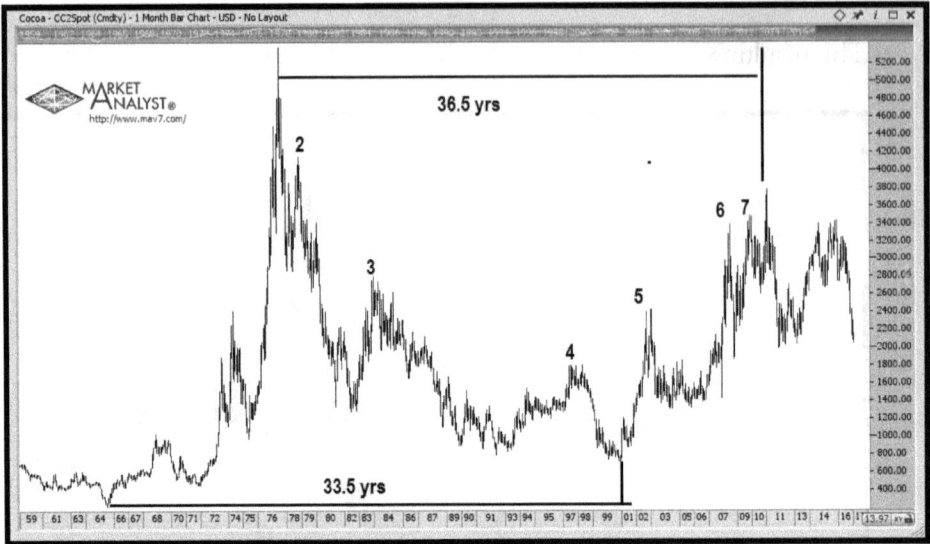

Figure 53 Monthly Cocoa chart

In Figure 53 we can see there were two major highs and they occurred **36.5 years** apart. In this long interval there were other major highs. So, in total over 36.5 years we count **8 highs**. Next we look for a span of time shorter than 36.5 years where there were two major bottoms. In this chart we note two major lows and they occurred **33.5 years** apart.

Now, we can engineer some mathematics.

36.5 years divided by 8 = 4.5625 years = 54.75 months.

33.5 years divided by 4.625 = 7.34 = 7 in round figures.

Therefore, 7 times 4.5625 = 31.93 = 383.25 months.

360 divided by 383.25 = 0.9393 degrees = 0.0163 radians (recall there are 2 pi radians in a circle).

360 divided by 54.75 = 6.575 degrees = 0.1147 radians.

Our general equation then becomes:

Y = cosine (A) + cosine (B); where A=0.0163 and B=0.1147

Y = cosine (0.0163 radians) + cosine (0.1147 radians)

Next we will set up a simple spreadsheet on a computer that takes the form as follows:

X	Y
1	Cosine (0.0163) + Cosine (0.1147)
2	Cosine (0.0327) + Cosine (0.2295)
3	Cosine (0.0491) + Cosine (0.3442)
4	Cosine (0.0655) + Cosine (0.4590)
5	Cosine (0.0891) + Cosine (0.5737)
And so on… for 700 rows	And so on…for 700 rows

The resulting X-Y plot looks like this:

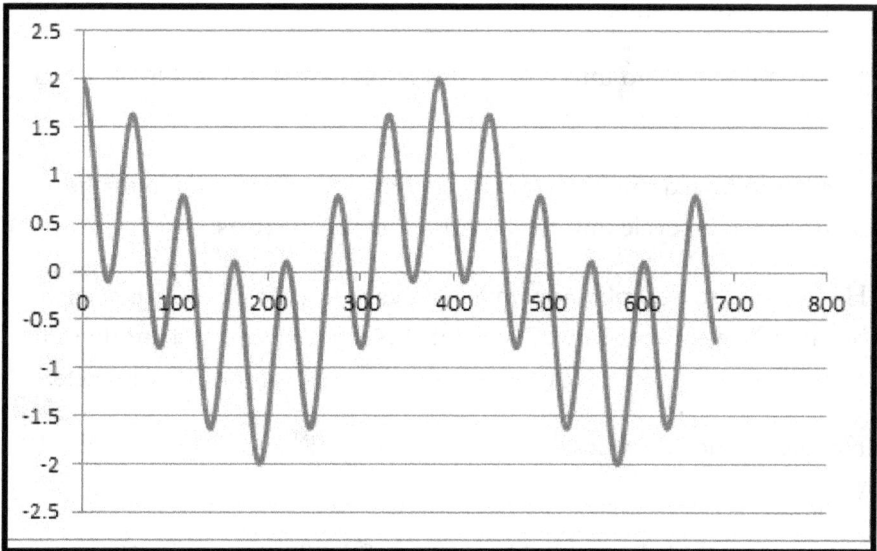

Figure 54 X-Y Plot of Cocoa Cosine Functions

Using a zero start point of the July 1977 high, I checked to see if the plot identified an inflection point at the peaks in October 2002 and November 2015. Indeed, the plot works well. several of these plotted intervals and they do indeed align reasonably well with inflection highs and lows on the historical monthly Oil chart. Note further that the data point

So as you can see, the Weston Model is not pin-point perfect, but it can handily let you know when a potential price inflection is looming. Combine this early warning with other astrological techniques such as McWhirter and you have the makings of a potent system. And remember, thanks to your hard efforts in studying this material, you now have these systems within your grasp. Think of the other traders, investors and Investment Advisors out there who do not.

In his day, Weston analyzed copious amounts of data from the Dow Jones Average. He applied his cosine Fourier mathematics and he came up with a general set of rules for the Dow. I have recently checked his model against the Dow Jones over the past number of years and I find that his model is still accurate.

I am not going to go into great elaboration here, but I will list for you his key points on the Dow.

Weston followed the 20 year cycle of Jupiter and Saturn. He further broke this long cycle into two components of 10 years.

He went on to describe how investors can expect a 20 month cycle to begin in November of the 1st year of the 10 year cycle and another 20 month cycle begins in November of the 5th year of the 10 year cycle.

He said 28 month cycles began in July of the 3rd and 7th years of the 10 year cycle.

A 10 month cycle begins in November of the 9th year of the 10 year cycle.

A 14 month cycle begins in September of the 10th year of the 10 year cycle.

The Saturn-Jupiter cycle forms a good part of what will be Course 3. So, at this point I will wrap up this Course and leave you to practice and deeply consider all that I have presented herein.

4. Encouraging Final Words

I think you will agree this has been a tough Course to navigate. What you have just been exposed to is some heavy-duty Astrology.

I have introduced you to the McWhirter method and detailed its three parts. Not exactly straight-forward, but with practice and chart study, you will soon get very skilled at it. I just wish that I had had a layman's manual like this one when I was struggling to learn her model.

I have introduced you to the complex work of Giacomo Albano. His work is rooted deep in classical Astrology. I think he is onto something with his approach. Just remember to keep it simple. Don't get too bogged down in the nuances of classical Astrology. All you are doing is making a judgement call. Is one Syzygy relatively better or worse than the next? Are there any nasty looking chart patterns in the horoscope wheel at the Syzygy?

Lastly, I have made you scramble to dust off your College mathematics textbook with the introduction to the Weston Model. Again, practice will help you to ultimately grasp this approach. It is not a pin-point precise model, so be sure to use it along with the other Astrology techniques you now know.

As you further embrace Financial Astrology as a valuable tool to assist you in your trading and investing activity, I further hope also that you will pause often to reflect on the deeper connection between the financial markets, Astrology and the emotions of mankind.

On that note, I will leave you with the 1951 words of astrologer Werner Hirsig:

"Astrology is a science in itself and contains an illuminating body of knowledge. It taught me many things, and I am greatly indebted to it. Geophysical evidence reveals the power of the stars and the planets in relation to the terrestrial. In turn, astrology reinforces this power to some extent. This is why astrology is like a life-giving elixir to mankind."

5. Glossary of Terms

Ascendant: One of four cardinal points on a horoscope, the Ascendant is situated in the East.

Aspect: The angular relationship between two planets measured in degrees.

Autumnal Equinox: (see Equinox) – That time of year when Sun is at 0 degrees Libra.

Conjunct: An angular relationship of 0 degrees between two planets.

Cosmo-biology: Changes in human emotion caused by changes in cosmic energy.

Descendant: One of four cardinal points on a horoscope, the Descendant is situated in the West.

Ephemeris: A daily tabular compilation of planetary and lunar positions.

Equinox: An event occurring twice annually, an equinox event marks the time when the tilt of the Earth's axis is neither toward or away from the Sun.

Exalted: various planets are dignified or made more powerful in certain signs.

Exile: various planets are humbled or made more weak in certain signs.

First Trade chart: A zodiac chart depicting the positions of the planets at the time a company's stock or a commodity future commenced trading on a recognized financial exchange.

First Trade date: The date a stock or commodity futures contract first began trading on a recognized exchange.

Full Moon: From a vantage point situated on Earth, when the Moon is seen to be 180 degrees to the Sun.

Geocentric Astrology: That version of Astrology in which the vantage point for determining planetary aspects is the Earth.

Grand Trine: a horoscope chart pattern of 3 planets where all are at 120 degrees to each other.

Grand Cross: see T-Square – two T-Square patterns together to make a square pattern.

Heliocentric Astrology: That version of Astrology in which the vantage point for determining planetary aspects is the Sun.

House: A 1/12th portion of the zodiac. Portions are not necessarily equal depending on the mathematical formula used to calculate the divisions.

In Terms: from the Ptolemaic astrology, meaning a defined point in a sign where a particular planet is 'happy'.

Lunar Eclipse: A lunar eclipse occurs when the Sun, Earth, and Moon are aligned exactly, or very closely so, with the Earth in the middle. The Earth blocks the Sun's rays from striking the Moon.

Lunar Month: (see Synodic Month.

Lunation: (see New Moon.)

Mid-Heaven: One of four cardinal points on a horoscope, the Mid-Heaven is situated in the South.

New Moon: From a vantage point situated on Earth, when the Moon is seen to be 0 degrees to the Sun.

North Node of Moon: The intersection points between the Moon's plane and Earth's ecliptic are termed the North and South nodes. Astrologers tend to focus on the North node and Ephemeris tables clearly list the zodiacal position of the North Node for each calendar day.

Orb: The amount of flexibility or tolerance given to an aspect.

Point of Thales: a horoscope chart pattern where two planets are 180 degrees apart. The angles formed with a 3rd planet are 60 and 90 degrees.

Retrograde motion: The apparent backwards motion of a planet through the zodiac signs when viewed from a vantage point on Earth.

Ruler: in the Zodiac, each sign is dominated over by a planet(s) called 'rulers'.

Sidereal Month: The Moon orbits Earth with a slightly elliptical pattern in approximately 27.3 days, relative to a fixed frame of reference.

Sidereal Orbital Period: The time required for a planet to make one full orbit of the Sun as viewed from a fixed vantage point on the Sun.

Siderograph: A mathematical equation developed by astrologer Donald Bradley in 1946 (By plotting the output of the equation against date, inflection points can be seen on the plotted curve. It is at these inflection points that human emotion is most apt to change resulting in a trend change on the Dow Jones or S&P 500 Index).

Solar Eclipse: A solar eclipse occurs when the Moon passes between the Sun and Earth and fully or partially blocks the Sun.

Solstice: Occurring twice annually, a solstice event marks the time when the Sun reaches its highest or lowest altitude above the horizon at noon.

Synodic Month: During a sidereal month (see Sidereal Month), Earth will revolve part way around the Sun thus making the average apparent time between one New Moon and the next New Moon longer than the sidereal month at approximately 29.5 days. This 29.5 day time span is called a Synodic Month or sometimes a Lunar Month.

Synodic Orbital Period: The time required for a planet to make one full orbit of the Sun as viewed from a fixed vantage point on Earth.

Syzygy: A pairing of planets. In the work of Giacomo Albano, generally regarded as a New Moon or a Full Moon.

T-Square: a horoscope pattern of 3 planets, where two are 180 degrees apart and each of those is 90 degrees to a third planet.

Vernal Equinox: That time of the year when Sun is at 0 degrees Aries.

Zodiac: An imaginary band encircling the 360 degrees of the planetary system divided into twelve equal portions of 30 degrees each.

Zodiac Wheel: A circular image broken into 12 portions of 30 degrees each. Each portion represents a different astrological sign.

6. Other Books By the Author

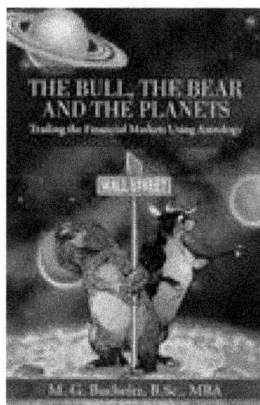

Once maligned by many, the subject of financial Astrology is now experiencing a revival as traders and investors seek deeper insight into the forces that move the financial markets.

The markets are a dynamic entity fueled by many factors, some of which we can easily comprehend, some of which are esoteric. This book introduces the reader to the notion that astrological phenomena can influence price action on financial markets and create trend changes across both short and longer term time horizons. From an introduction to the historical basics behind Astrology through to an examination of lunar Astrology and planetary aspects, the numerous illustrated examples in this book will introduce the reader the power of Astrology and its impact on both equity markets and commodity futures markets.

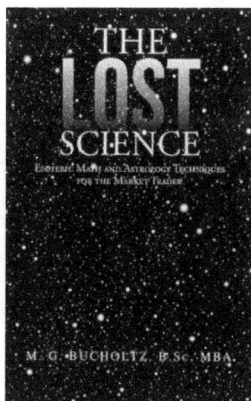

The financial markets are a reflection of the psychological emotions of traders and investors. These emotions ebb and flow in harmony with the forces of nature.

Scientific techniques and phenomena such as square root mathematics, the Golden Mean, the Golden Sequence, lunar events, planetary transits and planetary aspects have been used by civilizations dating as far back as the ancient Egyptians in order to comprehend the forces of nature.

The emotions of traders and investors can be seen to fluctuate in accordance with these forces of nature. Lunar events can be seen to align with trend changes on financial markets. Significant market cycles can be seen to align with planetary transits and aspects. Price patterns on stocks, commodity futures and market indices can be seen to conform to square root and Golden Mean mathematics.

In the early years of the 20th century the most successful traders on Wall Street, including the venerable W.D. Gann, used these scientific techniques and phenomena to profit from the markets. However, over the ensuing decades as technology has advanced, the science has been lost.

The Lost Science acquaints the reader with an extensive range of astrological and mathematical phenomena. From the Golden Mean and Fibonacci Sequence, to planetary transit lines and square roots through to an examination of lunar Astrology and planetary aspects, the numerous illustrated examples in this book will show the reader how these unique scientific phenomena impact the financial markets.

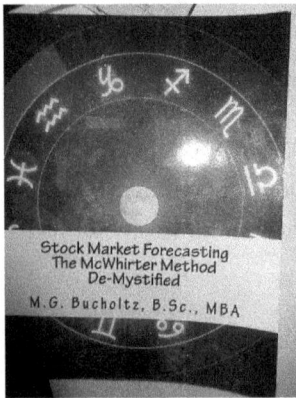

Stock Market Forecasting
The McWhirter Method
De-Mystified

M.G. Bucholtz, B.Sc., MBA

Very little is known about Louise McWhirter, except that in 1937 she wrote the book *McWhirter Theory of Stock Market Forecasting*.

In my travels to places as far away as the British Library in London, England to research financial Astrology, not once did I come across any other books by her. Not once did I find any other book from her era that even mentioned her name. All of this I find to be deeply mysterious. Whoever she was – she wrote only one book, and it was a powerful one that is as accurate today as it was back in 1937. The purpose of writing this book is suggested by the title itself – to de-mystify McWhirter's methodology - which is not exactly straightforward.

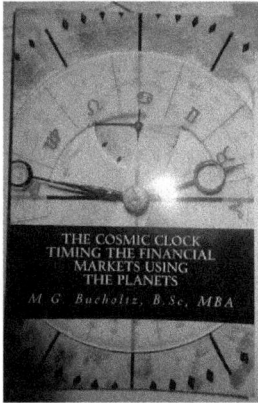

THE COSMIC CLOCK
TIMING THE FINANCIAL
MARKETS USING
THE PLANETS

M. G. Bucholtz, B.Sc, MBA

Can the movements of the Moon affect the stock market?

Are price swings on Crude Oil, Soybeans, the British pound and other financial instruments a reflection of planetary placements?

The answer to these questions is YES. Changes in price trends on the markets are in fact related to our changing emotions. Our emotions in turn are impacted by the changing events in our cosmos.

In the early part of the 20th century many successful traders on Wall Street, including the venerable W.D. Gann and the mysterious Louise McWhirter, understood that emotion was linked to the forces of the cosmos. They used astrological events and esoteric mathematics to predict changes in price trend and to profit from the markets.

However, in the latter part of the 20th century, the investment community has become more comfortable just relying on academic financial theory and the opinions of colorful television media personalities all wrapped up in a buy and hold mentality.

The Cosmic Clock has been written for traders and investors who are seeking to gain an understanding of the cosmic forces that influence emotion and the financial markets.

7. About The Author

Malcolm Bucholtz, B.Sc, MBA is a graduate of Queen's University Faculty of Engineering in Canada and Heriot Watt University in Scotland where he received an MBA degree. After working in Canadian industry for far too many years, Malcolm followed his passion for the financial markets by becoming an Investment Advisor/Commodity Trading Advisor with an independent brokerage firm in western Canada. Today, he resides in western Canada where he trades the financial markets using technical chart analysis, esoteric mathematics and the astrological principles outlined in this book.

Malcolm is the author of several books. His first book, *The Bull, the Bear and the Planets*, offers the reader an introduction to Financial Astrology and makes the case that there are esoteric and astrological phenomena that influence the financial markets. His second book, *The Lost Science*, takes the reader on a deeper journey into planetary events and unique mathematical phenomena that influence financial markets. His third book, *De-Mystifying the McWhirter Theory of Stock Market Forecasting* seeks to simplify and illustrate the McWhirter methodology. The Cosmic Clock is designed for people seeking to gain insight into the forces that influence the financial markets.

In addition, each year Malcolm releases a Financial Astrology Almanac. The 2017 Financial Astrology Almanac shows the reader the critical dates to watch for in 2017.

Malcolm maintains both a website (www.investingsuccess.ca) and a blog where he provides traders and investors with astrological insights into the financial markets. He also offers a bi-weekly **Astrology E-Alert** service where subscribers receive previews of pending astrological events that stand to influence markets.